Gift from

MW00951464

RESTORATION

THE HEARTBEAT OF GOD

WADE JENSEN, M. DIV.

WESTBOW
PRESS®
A DIVISION OF THOMAS NELSON
& ZONDERVAN

WestBow Press books may be ordered through booksellers or by contacting:

WestBow Press
A Division of Thomas Nelson & Zondervan
1663 Liberty Drive
Bloomington, IN 47403
www.westbowpress.com
844-714-3454

ISBN: 978-1-6642-4490-0 (sc)
ISBN: 978-1-6642-4491-7 (hc)
ISBN: 978-1-6642-4489-4 (e)

Library of Congress Control Number: 2021918906

Print information available on the last page.

WestBow Press rev. date: 10/21/2021

CONTENTS

Disclaimers and Terms of Use

The views expressed in this book are those of the author and do not reflect the official policy or position of the U.S. Government, the Department of Defense, or the U.S. Air Force. Additionally, the views do not reflect any position of the International Church of the Foursquare Church or any other entity, but are the author's alone.

No information in this book should be considered as counseling or legal advice. Your reliance upon information and content obtained by you at or through this publication is solely at your own risk. The author assumes no liability or responsibility for damage or injury to you, other persons, or property arising from any use of any product, information, idea, or instruction contained in the content or services provided to you through this book. Reliance upon information contained in this material is solely at the reader's own risk.

DEDICATION

To my parents, Jack and Diane Jensen. You have overcome a number of obstacles and circumstances in your life. I honor you as two of the best examples of what faith, perseverance, and forgiveness can lead to in a person's life. Long before there was "a little ditty about Jack and Diane," you committed to a life that was not easy but fulfilling.[1] You had six children raised with your values and have created a legacy all of us hope to pass down to the following generations. Love never fails, and neither does God.[2]

ENDORSEMENTS

Part of courage is knowing and believing that failures can be restored into successes. Knowing God can and does restore things shows His lovingkindness toward us all. Restoration gives us hope that things that were bad can be better in the future. Wade Jensen's book, *Restoration: The Heartbeat of God*, outlines for all of us just what restoration entails. It provides hope that things can be better, but Wade goes far beyond the personal level of restoring one's life and discusses churches, businesses, communities, states, and national levels of restoration. Even one person can change the negative trajectory toward a prosperous one. Jensen shows that while restoration can be instantaneous for one person, sometimes that restoration can take much longer as the vision of change is owned by others. Wade shows that with God, He is never late to His plan. We sometimes can be too early, but if we pause and listen to God, we'll line up with his timetable and arrive when He wants things to be restored.

Kevin Cullis
Author of *HWJDB How Would Jesus Do Business?* and *Wisdom, Work, Wealth: Find God's Purpose For Your Prosperity through Side Gigs, Startups, and Entrepreneurship*
International Speaker on Biblical Entrepreneurship.
www.hwjdb.com

Having known Wade for many years, it never surprises me when he writes something that is truly strait from the Father's heart. This book really captures how important restoration is to God. I believe that his insight is from the incredible relationship he has with his Heavenly Father. The timing of this book is spot on with what God is seeking for his children in this moment. If we want restoration in our personal lives, in the church, and in the nations of the world, it must be through divine order. Wade will help direct you to God's heart of restoration for you and your family. Enjoy the journey.

Pastor/Apostle Joshua Griffin
The Filling Station - Wellington Co.
www.wellingtonfillingstation.org

Wade Jensen is a man on fire, the very fire of God that burns in the eyes of Jesus to see people, cities, and nations restored. I once heard someone say that restoration is, "a returning to the original condition in the original position for the original purpose." That almost sounds too good to be true, especially if you need restoration! If you feel you are too far gone for God to restore you, this book is for you. If you believe the nation you live in is too far gone for God to bring restoration, this book is for you. I dare you to read this book and not only be restored, but join the "paraclete people!"

Brent Parker
Lead Pastor, The Gate
www.Churchatthegate.com

Wade Jensen understands the Heartbeat of God like very few people that I know. His search for God started over twenty years ago and has never lessened at all. He has an understanding and knowledge of Scripture that will both challenge you and create hunger in you for more.

Everyone needs to feel the Heartbeat of God. Let Wade take you to it. He walks there and will help you walk there too. Meeting Wade will change your life forever, but knowing him isn't his objective, but knowing God in a very personal, relational way is what Wade wants for you. Let your heart be drawn to God as you read the pages of this book.

Tony Portera
Pastor of The Potter's House
LaBarge, Wyoming
www.pottershouselabarge.com

If you're searching for practical resource for your life or your ministry, this book is for you. In *Restoration: The Heartbeat of God*, Wade passionately shares that restoration leads to fulfillment. He highlights that while we live in a broken world, God desires to see all things - including you and me - restored.

Jeremy A. Sparks
Hall of Fame Cowboy & Author, *Go West - 10 Principles That Guided My Cowboy Journey* - 2018 Christian Indie Book of the Year

ACKNOWLEDGMENTS

Without question, the first one I want to thank is God for rescuing me and restoring me to the proper path of life through Jesus, who has kept His promises through every step of my life. I praise Him for the Holy Spirit to pour out the insight and creativity to get this book produced. After huge setbacks, God demonstrated His ability to restore things I had not believed were possible at the time. I cannot fully express His faithfulness without producing another book!

I want to thank my wife, Heather, who has modeled both grace and restoration on a level going beyond human capacity. I also married above my pay grade and have someone gifted in English comprehension, able to make a book go from good to great. Through her encouragement and telling me to "write the thing," along with giving me space to create, this work is now coming to fruition four years after I started transforming this idea of restoration into a practical and tangible format anyone can follow. My children earned my thanks by praying me through to finishing. They gave up some playtime so I could get this book out at this crucial time in our culture.

I wish to thank my parents, Jack and Diane, for demonstrating what perseverance is and how restoration can be walked out, even in a marriage. I am grateful God worked through miraculous timing and ways to bring freedom. Along with my parents, I have been blessed with five siblings and I appreciate you all. And thanks to my marriage and our close church relationship, Roger and Clara Stevens have been present for the entire family more often than I can count. Their example to the body of Christ has made news in heaven. I must also mention Ed and Glenda Espinoza, who have been instrumental in my faith becoming a reality. Thank you,

Ed, for leading me to Christ and being available at pivotal moments in my life.

I must recognize some key people who helped restore me after some significant upheaval. Janice Seney, who went to be with the Lord in 2019, gave me a prophetic word in 1995, which has stuck with me for the last twenty-five years, and she happened to be present at critical junctures in my life up until three months before she passed away. Pastors Brent and Tani Parker were instrumental in getting me on my road to "destiny." The pun is intentional, as it's the name of the church they pastored for more than twenty years. Through Janice Seney and the Parkers, I was led to the International Church of the Foursquare Gospel, which I have appreciated greatly.

Mark and Mona Hirsch, who owned the Christian bookstore in Rapid City when we lived there, gave sage advice, keeping me on the path of life. Mark stated, "You will be a leader, and you will not be perfect. The grace you give now will be the grace you receive later." Nearly twenty years later, I cannot mention how many times this has been true. Bob and Cheria Guier, through Restoring the Foundations (RTF) Ministry, executed a thorough overhaul over a Christmas break to fit my wife and me in their schedule. Bob has mentored me in so many ways over the last twenty-five years. His friendship, humor, and authenticity have been priceless. My "five-fold" friend, John McDowell, has been there for my greatest triumphs and knows the deepest wounds I have ever experienced. I have appreciated our lasting friendship over the decades now.

I have been with some key leaders who shaped me as a disciple of Christ. First, Pastors Tony and Gwenette Portera in LaBarge, Wyoming, allowed some mentoring to happen, and most people would do well to follow their example. Pastor Tony said that he could teach me everything he knew in ten minutes, but the learning has continued for more than twenty-five years. Pastor J.R. and Yvonne Polhemus treated us like family. I am thankful for their love, encouragement, and support from before my Iraq deployment to a transition we did not see coming. Pastors Joshua and Jennifer Griffin affirmed the gifts and talents of our entire family! Their view of leadership and how the Body of Christ works must spread like wildfire, and I am glad God had our paths intersect. My mentor in Cheyenne, Pastor Bill Curran, has been the primary motivator for me to write, following my wife. He did not accept excuses and was willing to give the left boot of correction, free of charge. Even at age eighty-seven at the time, he was quite effective.

I am grateful for God placing my family and me in the same place as Mike and Jody Skinner. I am truly thankful for a connection in Iraq, leading me to the right editor for this work. Jody ensured "every smidgen mattered." Additionally, Kevin Cullis delivered helpful insight into making the final version of this book even better. I want to thank David Morrell, who took the time to visit with me in Iraq to encourage me to pursue writing. I want to thank Dr. Douglas Groothuis for all his books, his teaching, and his insight.

I want to thank Rick Joyner for discussing restoration with Rev. Jim Bakker after purchasing the Heritage Property in Fort Mill, South Carolina. That particular episode of *The Jim Bakker Show*, along with my personal and professional experience, ignited the ideas for this book.

Finally, I would like to thank all of the staff at Westbow Press in their diligence in helping to get this book out in its final form. In particular, I wish to thank Leandra Drummy who was always the faithful one I could count on, even in the midst of the COVID conditions. And to all the others behind the scenes who I have not mentioned, know that God witnessed your partnership and support even if I did not mention it here. With your assistance, the seeds of restoration will hopefully become a reality.

PREFACE

What would a template for restoration look like if you could create it? Would you begin with a simple graphic design or have a ten-thousand-word written plan that lays out the details? Whether simple or complicated, no one has perfected the art of restoration, at least not from a human perspective. However, everyone loves seeing a restored car, a restored house, or a restored piece of antique furniture. Within our framework, something deep within appreciates the restoration process.

When it comes to restoring something that was lost, can we ever get it back? Can we get the person back? How can we get back on the track of wholeness? What does authentic restoration look like to us? Things can be restored to us, but does that change our heart condition? This book is for people who want to not only restore what was lost but also hold to the higher expectation that God's desire is for a complete restoration, which we will see.[3] The point is to help people realize God is a good God and not the author of confusion.[4] If our hearts can be disciplined so that a confident expectation can be reprogrammed into us, then we may observe a restoration process occur within our own lives.

Besides restoring something lost, God has four areas of focus where He wants to see us all achieve the highest restoration possible and, above all, operate out of love. The four areas of focus for restoration are things stolen, things killed, things destroyed, and things to overcome. If love is the motivation behind restoration, it will be taken to completion and not done in a half-hearted manner. Now keep in mind, Jesus told us to "love our enemies."[5] What greater love can we have for our enemies than restoring them to a place more significant than they were before? In some families and faith communities, the "enemy" can be the person who hurt us. As Americans, we have observed our nation restoring the nations who were our sworn enemies. But the restoration of our enemies can carry more authority, both naturally and spiritually, than we can be aware of in the present. The bottom line is this: love must be the main motivational factor in all of our actions.

On a spiritual level, there is a thief who comes to steal, kill, and destroy.[6] But Jesus said He came to give us life more abundantly.[7] So it is imperative to know who is on our side and who is not. Beyond loss, any place where the enemy robbed us marks a great place to start searching for how God wants to restore it, whatever "it" is. This theft can be physical, mental, emotional, material, or spiritual. We can make a list of what the enemy stole and start going after every item requiring restoration.

When it comes to someone dying, we do not have a 100 percent resurrection rate—not yet anyway. But some other things killed off—like dreams, desires, visions, or legacies—can be resurrected, even on behalf of someone who was lost. Clausewitz's *On War* was published posthumously by his wife because she saw value in everything he wrote.[8] Some things get restored by people who follow after us.

After destruction, following overwhelming grief, the desire to rebuild rises to the surface. God created us in His likeness and image. God's willingness moved toward restoration for humanity and the entire world system even before the Fall happened. So if God wanted to restore everything, humanity would have this similar inclination. Once again, the destruction can be in several subjective or objective areas, but the desire to see the final restoration moves from somewhere deep inside. I was raised in what is called not only "Tornado Alley" but "Hail Alley." Do you have any idea what softball-sized hail coming down for thirty minutes will do to a car or house? Some people have seen more significant hail following a tornado that wipes out the entire town. But many of us in the United States and around the world have another reference point for restoration being necessary.

The COVID Condition

I grew up reading *Space 1999*, thinking of a much different 2020 when I was ten years old. The restoration of houses, businesses, communities, and cities comes to the forefront of our thinking, especially if it is *our* home, business, or community. Then relationships need healing and restoration. Ethnic groups must come together and work on restoration if we desire to see a nation stand, let alone get rebuilt. Some people would like decency, honor, and respect for our fellow human to return. Without a doubt, some practical application has to be available, or the biblical foundation and concept of restoration will not occur at the pace or level we desire.

Thankfully, restoration is at the foundation of God's design and desire. Throughout human history, God has chosen to reveal patterns in the form of pictures and words. When humanity has chosen to follow this pattern, the restoration has a way of transforming everything, from a mindset to a municipality. I want this reference to be a spark that ignites the creativity that God has placed within you to transform your sphere of influence, beginning with you.

FOREWORD

Wade and Heather Jensen attended the church I pastored in Castle Rock, Colorado, for several years. We got to know them and love them as they were a vital part of our church and our home group. They were involved in our prayer shield and prayed for myself, my family, and our church. I also deeply appreciated the sacrifices Wade made in service to our country as a chaplain in the Air Force. He brought a spiritual dimension of a personal relationship with God through Jesus Christ, which is so vital to all, but especially to our military. Wade was not afraid to go on dangerous missions, risking life and limb, to help those in traumatic situations.

Restoration: The Heartbeat of God is a book that literally exposes God's heart in a powerful way. Wade demonstrates how God is deeply involved in our personal restoration as well as restoration in our families and communities. As a history major in college, I was particularly interested and informed by the insight that Wade brought about God's involvement in World War II (WWII). Unfortunately, in most history books, God's influence is omitted. But Wade provides the missing ingredient in a revelatory way.

My hope is that as you read this book, you will be moved as I was. It helped me to see some of the restoration I have experienced in my life from God's perspective and encouraged me where I have not seen that full restoration. I believe the principles of this book can be applied to all facets of a person's life regardless of their career or professional endeavor. This is the kind of book you will want to pass on to your friends. You will not only be blessed by it but be a blessing.

Love,
Pastor JR Polhemus
Pastor Emeritus, The Rock, Castle Rock, CO

1

IT STARTED WITH A CUT

The greater the restoration, the more significantly
history and culture get affected.

Lying facedown on the operating table, I had a lot of thoughts going through my mind. All those thoughts melted away as I felt the scalpel run down my back, telling me the local anesthetic had not taken effect. Jerking or moving in any way would only have made things worse, so I yelled out to the operating team that I was not numb. The surgeon stopped and jabbed a needle in several places, which I could feel as well. This scenario is certainly not expected, especially in one's twenties.

I could not understand how I had ended up with skin cancer. I was fair skinned, so I was careful to use sunscreen whenever I was outdoors. After undergoing the pain, treatment, and numerous scans, almost all cancer survivors desire the old normal, not the new normal. How can life be better than it was? For some, an internal fortitude drives them to surpass their previous state of being and become better. Cancer survivors exemplify this, but people surviving adverse circumstances gain a new perspective in life. The big question is "Can restoration truly happen?" This question arises any time something tragic happens, especially if some kind of loss is involved.

By definition, *restoration* refers to:

> An act of restoring or the condition of being restored: ***
> a bringing back to a former position or condition:

reinstatement, restoration of peace; a restoration to an unimpaired or improved condition; a representation or reconstruction of the original form.[9]

Within this definition, the word _peace_ in the form of _shalom_ literally means nothing is missing or nothing is broken and is defined as wholeness or completeness.[10] From these definitions, if one wonders what restoration looks like, this is it.

Restoration can also be an art form, where the broken pieces are taken by the artist to make an object whole again. The person may look like the Japanese art called _kintsugi_, meaning "golden joinery."[11] This art technique takes things that are broken, such as a pot or cup, and places them together again using an adhesive with gold flakes. The idea behind this reflects that the restored object has even more beauty than the original.[12] When it comes to a person, this is what God sees. Christians are marked with the restorative work of Christ in their lives. When we allow the "gold" of His grace to fill in the cracks and achieve wholeness, we place something beautiful in God's eyes back into use as a vessel unto Him.

Art is truly in the eye of the beholder. The way kintsugi comes together can leave one breathless, like seeing Niagara Falls or Mount Rushmore for the first time. The personal events from my life do not take a chronological order but are the broken pieces in my life that God picked up at different times and inserted His gold.

PUBLIC HUMILIATION AND CURSES

For some people, pain, brokenness, and scars are invisible and can be extremely challenging to overcome. This spectrum of adversity and loss is also difficult to measure because only an individual and God understand the hurt and bitterness that secured a place inside. Scripture declares, "No heart knows its own bitterness, and no one shares its joy."[13] I know others have had personal experiences worse than mine because I have heard them as a chaplain. But I will share two that were exceedingly painful for me.

I grew up in a small town with fewer than forty kids at my grade level. In second grade, during music class, I dropped my eraser on the floor, so

I bent down and picked it up. When I sat back up at my desk, this male teacher's hand came across my face, almost knocking me back out of the desk. He said nothing. Then he slapped me across the face again. I was a good kid and a good student. To this day, I do not know why he slapped me that hard in the middle of class.

I did not tell my parents about this incident. Due to the embarrassment I felt along with the pain, I had strong negative associations when it came to anything about music as a class to take. Since I grew up in a small town, he was the only music teacher for elementary school. When my parents asked me to learn an instrument or go into band class, I refused and even threw a fit, so I did nothing with voice or instruments or music in general, even though I honestly loved music.

Being around people who hear the voice of God, I had one person tell me that a musical gift was lying dormant inside me. I could not be transported back to my childhood to learn to sing or go back and become proficient at an instrument, so I felt lost about how I could wake that dormant gift out of that slumber. I have forgiven that teacher, but I have not forgotten the pain. Yet, God has not forgotten either, and all of my children have a musical gifting. The gold of God's glory has been showing up in my cracks.

Public humiliation did not stop with the music teacher. In 2001, I had a minister feel the need to teach me a lesson because of a book I shared with people in the church. During our annual prophetic conference, everything he perceived I had done wrong over the four years leading up to that point in my life came to public knowledge in the foyer of the hotel conference center with a crowd around us. This filled me with shame. I did not know how I would show up in a church again, let alone be involved in ministry. I cannot blame-shift (BS) here either. I hesitate to share this because God truly has healed me and restored me through some key people. Of all things, this incident redirected me to the calling I had as a chaplain. More gold had been inserted to fill the cracks.

As a chaplain, I hear too many stories of people who have wounds from a minister or priest and vow they cannot return to a church setting. No matter how broken the pieces are, God can heal the wound and restore things better than the original. David became a great king because he served under a prideful and demented King Saul. God's purpose for restoration extends to every person, both to the offender and the offended.

Thankfully, I have not had another episode of that skin cancer, with the feeling of a scalpel going down my back, or public humiliation. These experiences instilled an awareness of adversity. After graduating from seminary in 2005, I began reading accounts of people who overcame great odds to achieve breakthroughs in faith, freedom, finances, and science. Whether the stories were real or fictional, they inspired me not to remain the same.

BARRACUDA

© Photo by Ted Johnson

I have another passion due to the vehicles that my parents had when I was learning to drive. I am happy to say that the first vehicle I learned to drive had a standard transmission. It may have been rusted out in some places, but not many people can say they learned to drive in a 1956 Chevy stepside truck. The steering wheel was huge, like you would see in a semi-truck today. Thankfully, there are plenty of dirt roads in western South Dakota that allow fourteen-year-olds the space and lack of traffic to practice the techniques of starting, stopping, steering, and shifting.

In addition to the old Chevy truck, my mom bought a 1965 Plymouth Fury II, which ended up being the car that I took ownership of at sixteen and drove through high school. The convertible Sport Fury had been the Indianapolis 500 pace car in 1965, but my mom bought the practical four-door sedan with a 318-cubic-inch V8, which became an excellent practical car for hauling kids to school, since I was the oldest of six.

I was allowed to start driving at fourteen because I had a job, working at a Coast to Coast Hardware store. My dad asked, "How are you going to pay for the car, the gas, and the insurance when you drive?" Everything was great for the first two years. However, it did not take this young man long to figure out that maintenance wasn't necessarily cheap when the alternator went out—typical for that age of a car. When I bought the car at sixteen, I took responsibility for everything. Do you know how much parts cost for a car more than twenty years old? That incident made me realize that the dream of restoring Mom's old car was not realistic because it was too expensive, and it was not the Sport Fury that car enthusiasts appreciated anyway.

Thanks to my familiarity with older vehicles, I had quite the opportunity while attending language school in Monterey, California. A man needed some cash and listed his car for sale at a whopping $1,300. For an E-2 soldier at age nineteen, that is what is known as affordable! Since I offered cash, I made the deal at $1,100. This would be crazy today, considering it was a 1965 Plymouth Barracuda, Golden Anniversary Edition. It was gold in and gold out, with a V8 and the original air-conditioning that still worked!

The Barracuda delivered excitement, enjoyment, and some interesting looks. The hard part was not just maintaining this car but restoring it with the right parts. While I was stationed in North Carolina, I had one memorable success. One of the original rims had become warped over time, so I had to find another one. This Barracuda had all original five-lug, thirteen-inch rims. Do you want to know how rare that is? Before the internet, the search involved several phone calls and many trips to different scrapyards in the region. One Saturday, I found a property with several classic cars on it that I "happened" to pass. The sign said that it was open, so I pulled in. I asked the gentleman if he had any Barracudas on the property, and he said he had two! As we walked back, we came to the cars . . . with no rims on the vehicles. However, I asked to look in one of the trunks that was not open. As we opened the trunk, there was one rim with the tire still on it.

Restoration to the original condition can be time-consuming or even painful, but the finished product is always worth it.

THE DETRIMENTAL SIDE OF DEPLOYMENT

I have been honored and privileged to serve our nation in both the army and air force, as enlisted and as a chaplain through a direct commission, respectively. Before deploying to Al Udeid Air Base in 2013, I had to get the anthrax vaccination series. The anthrax shots always hurt and make a person flare up in several ways, but one time was different.

I happened to have one shot in the series before my drill weekend with the Air National Guard. As we came into drill weekend, I could hardly move my left shoulder, and my noncommissioned officer in charge (NCOIC) superintendent happened to be a nurse on the civilian side. He looked at my shoulder and was immediately alarmed. I had a huge red patch, which he proceeded to outline with a permanent marker. He said if it became any worse, I needed to go get it examined.

The next day, the cellulitis had expanded beyond the outline. A military provider checked me out and said I needed to go to a provider off base and get some antibiotics. Providentially, the person who had given me the anthrax shot had told me, "If you have any shortness of breath or feel off, just go to the emergency room." I did go home with some antibiotics, but two days after I got home from drill weekend, I woke up at 2:25 a.m. and felt short of breath. Plus, I felt abnormal, like something was way off-line in my body.

I flipped on the light in the bathroom to see dark red streaks in the veins going down to my left hand. At this point, I moaned a little bit because that hand, along with my left shoulder, hurt to the touch. My wife woke up and said, "You are going to the ER, aren't you?" Since we had three little kids, I told her that I was coherent and could drive myself to the hospital. When I arrived at the ER, the nurse assessed me, and she admitted me quickly when my blood pressure came back at 160/104. They had trouble getting an IV in but finally managed in my right bicep—and I am usually an "easy poke."

I had nearly gone septic, so I had to stay in the hospital for two days for IV antibiotics. I was confused about why a nephrologist came to see me and why they measured my fluids, but it turned out that my kidneys had started to shut down, which I didn't find out until eighteen months later at another appointment. The nephrologist released me on the condition that I would have a follow-up appointment, which I stated I would do at the VA Hospital. However, five days after this episode, I not only had constant pain in my left shoulder, but I also started having pain in my lower back, the other shoulder, and both hip joints.

I wish it had stopped there. After a month out of the hospital, my eyes kept itching, and my eyelashes started coming out. Within two weeks, I had no eyelashes! Then I felt sick again. I went to the doctor, and sure enough, I had a respiratory infection, so I received more antibiotics. I overcame that infection just in time to fly out on my deployment to Al Udeid, near the Persian Gulf.

During my 197 days overseas, I served, but the pain became worse. Additionally, my immune system had become suppressed since the last Anthrax vaccine. Hives would break out on my left shoulder where I received the shot, and within forty-eight hours, I would have some kind of illness. In this time frame, I had strep throat, three respiratory infections, and shingles. None of these are familiar to a man in his forties.

When I returned, I was evaluated, but no one believed that all of these previous symptoms were linked to an adverse reaction to the anthrax series. However, the allergy specialist could not find another explanation as to why I still had histamine breakouts in the same location seven years later. To combat the breakouts, I must be on allergy medications for the rest of my life, short of a miracle. Even with allergy medication, hives still occur on the left shoulder every six weeks, followed by my immune system shutting down within two days. I have combatted this through my own experience of taking 10,000 mg of vitamin C when they appear.

I also gained twenty-five pounds in six months after the Anthrax shot. The rheumatologist who saw me about the pain issues ordered labs and found out my thyroid was no longer functioning. He could not explain what was causing my pain because the results came back negative for everything else.

As a chaplain, I now have sympathy and empathy for anyone dealing with chronic pain, health issues that cannot be explained, the doctor not believing their stories, or conditions that cannot be cured short of a miracle. After six years, I still ask questions in the military and VA health systems to see any change. Since I have been miraculously healed three times in my life, I will seek prayer, whenever I can, for healing, or receive prayer if someone wants to pray for me. I want restoration badly enough that I will keep contending for it.

THE PHOENIX RISING

Throughout grade school and high school, I had trouble reading. Thanks to a teacher who offered different kinds of literature classes in high school, I grasped reading through Greek mythology and science fiction. The theme of restoration transcended the ages. The greater the restoration, the more significantly history and culture get impacted.

From Greek mythology, the phoenix rising out of the ashes stood out to me in a profound way. The phoenix "has been a symbol of destruction, rebirth, and renewal throughout several eras and cultures."[14] This flaming bird had a way of coming back that would puzzle the person who thought it was gone. As I read about the phoenix, something ignited within me when restoration followed total annihilation.

A spark of hope appeared. When hope gets renewed, faith builds up. Hope ignites and faith increases because something is working beyond the circumstances. Whether the root cause of restoration is natural or supernatural, the thrill of witnessing complete restoration has captured the gaze and imagination of many through the ages. We can imagine that we take the place of that phoenix. We all can rise, like a phoenix, out of the ashes.

THE GREATEST BOOK ON RESTORATION

The book with the most stories reflecting the theme of restoration is the Bible. I had read through the entire Bible by the time I was twenty-two, but the stories did not stand out to me until I started studying the book and allowed the Author and the book to speak to me. From the beginning, restoration is a theme woven through the narrative of almost every book and letter.

If a person gets excited about a car, a house, or antique furniture being restored, how much more should we be excited about a person being restored? According to the definition of peace observed earlier, how exciting would it be to see the entire person and all facets of life completely whole? I am talking about spiritual, mental, physical, and financial wholeness. Truly, if nothing is missing or broken, what facet of a person's life would not be touched?

The intent of this project is to examine the importance of restoration and its implications to every person, community, sphere of society, and nation. There is a wealth of examples we can use to see restoration at work, and we will focus on several of them to understand how significant restoration is—not just to us but also to God. Then this concept of restoration shall be applied in context to various facets, beginning with individual lives.

Allow this resource to work in you and through you to embrace the process of restoration and be a conductor of restoration within your area of influence.

Points to Ponder

1. Can restoration truly happen?
2. What would it look like to have nothing missing and nothing broken?
3. How can something be restored after such hurt and loss?
4. Now, a restoration to the original can be time-consuming or even painful, but the finished product is always worth it. What comes to your mind that needs restoration?
5. How important is restoration to you?
6. How would you view restoration if God was in charge?
7. If nothing is missing or broken, what facet of a person's life would not be touched?

2

THE FOUNDATION FOR RESTORATION

And that He may send Jesus, the Christ appointed for you, *apokatastasis*
whom heaven must receive until the period of restoration
of all things about which God spoke by the mouth of his
holy prophets from ancient time.[15]

When anyone considers the themes woven throughout Scripture, two
come to the forefront. The redemption of humanity is the primary
theme. The second theme repeated through the Bible is restoration. Like a
rope with three strands, God is woven through every aspect of redemption
with the restoration of all that was lost. When proper exegesis is applied
to the Bible in context, the nuggets of truth can be extracted like a gold
vein in a mine.

The central aspect of biblical interpretation comes from the context of
the passage within its narrative and historical background. The big idea
is to get the author's intent. Ultimately, the author is God, so one of the
truths that Christians adhere to is the inerrancy of Scripture in its original
transcription.[16] Precedence plays a key role, which is where the "law of
first mention" is established.[17] The law of first mention indicates the first
time a term or theme is used, it carries significance throughout the rest
of Scripture. Considering these aspects, I want to not only examine a few
words and passages in particular here but also expand on two passages that

demonstrate the kindness, power, love, and justice of God. Since the law of first mention is so important, consider what is mentioned in the first chapter of Genesis.

IT STARTED WITH A SEED

From the beginning, "God created the heavens and the earth."[18] The very first mention of God has Him initiating everything, and what He begins, He will complete. Then the very next verse is the first mention of the Spirit of God. He is "moving," or hovering, indicating He is ready and willing to do the works of God by the Word of God. The term *moving* is the Hebrew word רָחַף, *rachaph*, which means "to be moved, affected, especially with tender love, hence to cherish."[19] The Spirit of God cherishes creation and cherishes the opportunity to affect creation with the will and Word of God. It is not just a matter of a willingness to do this; the Spirit of God loves doing this. This is vitally important to know for all the Scriptures.

What is so significant about a seed? The Scripture states, "And the earth brought forth vegetation, plants yielding seed after their kind, and trees bearing fruit, with seed in them, after their kind; and God saw that it was good. And there was evening, and there was morning, a third day."[20] Now consider this: there was no destruction due to sin in the world at this point in creation, so why would plants have seeds? The word *seed*, עֶזַר, *zera* in Hebrew, means "That which is scattered, but can also mean *harvest* since people gathered seeds or fruit for food."[21] In order for a seed to produce life, the actual seed must die. What would this indicate? The theology is also in the literature. Seeds are mentioned with the creation of plant life on the third day. They produce after their own kind. So when the Bible mentions that Jesus rose on the third day, what did the author(s) have in mind and what was the reference for?[22]

When it came to the test of obedience to the first man and woman, God placed two trees in the Garden of Eden among all the other plant life that were set apart. "The two trees were the Tree of Life and the Tree of the Knowledge of Good and Evil."[23] Adam was commanded not to eat from the latter, but he could have eaten from the former.[24] Take note—the "test" was over something that produced seeds. Each tree produced after its own kind. Interestingly, the curse on the ground that followed Adam's disobedience of consuming from the Tree of Knowledge produced "thorns, thistles, and toil," which any novice farmer can guess was not good.[25]

As a sign of restoration, "the LORD God made garments of skin for Adam and his wife, and clothed them."[26] Now for the garments to be *incorrect* made, an animal or animals had to die. Blood had to be shed. This is the first mention of any blood being spilled or death occurring to something. Since Adam had not needed clothing before this, he did not know how to make items, so God fashioned the vestments. Just as Adam could not begin to make a way for survival, let alone restoration, God initiated a new era that would require sacrifice to get humanity and creation back to the original blueprint.

Due to this act of disobedience, everything came under a curse, including the serpent, humankind, and all of creation. However, in the midst of the curse, a promise is given. Once again, seeds are referenced: "And I will put enmity between you and the woman, and between your seed and her seed; he shall bruise you on the head, and you shall bruise him on the heel."[27] Within this verse, some interesting language is used. First, *seed* is normally referring to the man, so if the seed is not coming *from* man, it can only come from God. Much later in time and Scripture, a woman named Mary conceived by the sowing of the Holy Spirit, not by the "seed" of man. Jesus became the "fruit of her womb" and the seed that produced the fulfillment of this passage.[28]

RESTORATION FORETOLD THROUGH NARRATIVE AND DECLARATIONS

Following the narrative concerning creation and the destruction of God's divine order, a restoration of God's intent comes out of the flood, when God declared, "While earth remains, seedtime and harvest, and cold and heat, and summer and winter, and day and night shall not cease."[29] Notice that a reference to seeds came in God's declaration of order being reestablished. God also established a covenant between Noah and all living things that survived the flood, stating He would not destroy the whole earth with a flood again.[30]

God spoke again to another man named Abram (who became Abraham after a name change initiated by God) and declared, "And I will make you a great nation, and I will bless you, and make your name great; and so you shall be a blessing; and I will bless those who bless you and the one who curses you I will curse. And in you all the families of the earth shall be blessed."[31] Now this is quite the declaration! How can all of the families of the earth be blessed in him? Some of us already know this answer, but some other points must be made before I go there. Once again, the theology is in the literature. Even Abram's own family is blessed soon after this declaration.

Lot, Abram's nephew, had separated from him due to both men's vast amount of livestock. The logistics of finding enough grazing for all the animals was too difficult. Abram gave Lot the first choice of the land to take. Lot chose to go east and settled in the valley of Sodom.

A short time later, Lot was captured during a war between kings, including the king of Sodom. When Abram heard of it, he went to war in order to free his nephew.[32] This narrative becomes the first mention of something being taken and then restored, including Abram's nephew, Lot, and the possessions of the other kings in the war. In the midst of this restoration, Abram receives another blessing from the first priest of God Most High ever mentioned in Scripture.

A priest named "Melchizedek, king of Salem," blessed Abram and said, "Blessed be Abram of God Most High, Possessor of heaven and earth; and blessed be God Most High, who has delivered your enemies into your hand."[33] Within the name of the first priest mentioned, two other terms came to the forefront for the first time. *Melchizedek* means "king of righteousness," and *Salem* is the Hebrew word שָׁלֵם, *shalom,* or "peace," used as a proper name.[34] What is righteousness? *Righteousness* is the Hebrew word צֶדֶק, *tsedeq,* meaning "right standing, justice, in relation to rulers or authority," or in this instance, with God.[35] The Hebrew word שָׁלֵם, *shalom,* means "whole, perfect, just (as in weight)."[36] Considering both of these names, they are also deep theological terms that carry significance throughout Scripture. I wonder where the blessing upon Abram was going if a man named with these two terms came to meet him?

One of the most powerful narratives on restoration occurred with the life of Joseph, the son of Jacob (Israel), the son of Isaac, the son of

Abraham (formerly Abram). So much happened in the life of Joseph that I have dedicated chapter 6 to this man and his life. However, the lineage is important, and the blessings and declarations Jacob issued over all his sons prior to his death are very important. The most important declaration Jacob made referred to Judah, which stated, "The scepter shall not depart from Judah, nor the ruler's staff from between his feet, until Shiloh comes and to him shall be the obedience of the peoples."[37] The Israelites had no ruler at this time, and "obedience of the peoples" described the exact opposite of what humanity had been, as told in the first book of the law.

The author of Genesis perceived something that had not happened yet, indicating some kind of transformation was coming. The reference to "peoples" does not just refer to Israelites but to all the people. How would that happen? Someone needed to restore all of humanity to an ability to obey God. But wait—there is more.

> Following a long line of ancestors, a man was born to the tribe of Judah named David. Like Joseph, he began in obscurity, but he was raised up and chosen by God. David lost everything more than once, but God restored him. Two declarations over David hold profound significance. After King Saul failed, the prophet Samuel declared this:
>
> "You have acted foolishly; you have not kept the commandment of the LORD your God, which He commanded you, for now the LORD would have established your kingdom over Israel forever. But now your kingdom shall not endure. The LORD has sought out for Himself a man after His own heart, and the LORD has appointed him as ruler over His people, because you have not kept what the LORD commanded you."[38]

Think of what King Saul lost due to his disobedience. Going clear back to Adam, this had to be one of the greatest losses any person had suffered due to disobedience. But this declaration fulfills what Jacob declared over the tribe of Judah in the book of Genesis, stating that David's lineage would be established forever.[39] Samuel said that the Lord was looking for someone after His own heart. So what was in David's heart? Clearly, David caught God's attention somehow.

Nothing reveals the heart like poetry or music. Thanks to providence and Scripture, we have a very good idea what King David's heart was like from reading the psalms. No matter how much or little people know about the Bible, Psalm 23 is well known in many circles. Within this "shepherd's psalm," the first verse states, "The LORD is my shepherd, I shall not be in want."[40] In Hebrew, the latter part of this sentence is "I shall lack nothing." What would your life look like if you lacked nothing at all? David continued within this psalm, saying, "He restores my soul."[41] This kind of restoration can only happen supernaturally. So, if David's heart was after God's own heart, what do you think is on God's heart?

David wrote a prayer and petition as a psalm after Nathan the prophet confronted him following his adultery, betrayal, deceit, and murder. Even after all of this, King David wrote, "Create in me a clean heart and renew a steadfast spirit within me. Do not cast me away from Your presence, and do not take Your Holy Spirit from me. Restore to me the joy of Your salvation, and sustain me with a willing spirit."[42] King David understood who could clean his heart, renew a steadfast spirit, and restore the joy of God's salvation. Clearly, only God can do anything like this. If this is God's heart, how would He bring it to pass?

Throughout the Scriptures, up to the period of the Roman Empire, numerous prophets foretold of a time that would come when everything that was lost would be restored. The way in which restoration would be realized became a good mystery, since each historical prophet only had a part of the picture revealed to them. Some of the passages that have been recorded direct the reader willing to explore the Scriptures to see that something valuable can be pieced together. Consider the following passages and the times when they were written.

The prophet Isaiah was sent by God at a time when the depravity of Israel probably matched the times of Noah, where it had become so evil that God could not stand it. Isaiah stated, "Woe to those who call evil good, and good evil; who substitute darkness for light and light for darkness; who substitute bitter for sweet, and sweet for bitter!"[43] Does that sound similar to anything you currently experience? Yet, in the midst of these dark times, Isaiah saw times of restoration that sounded impossible. He recorded this passage:

> But there will be no more gloom for her who was in anguish; in earlier times He treated the land of Zebulun and the land of Naphtali with contempt, but later on He shall make it glorious, by the way of the sea, on the other side of Jordan, Galilee of the Gentiles. The people who walk in darkness will see a great light; those who live in a dark land, the light will shine of them … For a child will be born to us; and the government will rest on His shoulders; and His name will be called Wonderful Counselor, Mighty God, Eternal Father, Prince of Peace. There will be no end to the increase of His government or of peace, on the throne of David and over his kingdom, to establish it and to uphold it with justice and righteousness from then on and forevermore. The zeal of the LORD of hosts will accomplish this.[44]

Can you believe that this is the same prophet who quoted "woe to them" in their ultimate form of depravity just four chapters prior to this? In the Scripture just quoted, numerous gems refract out to passages we will cover, involving light, righteousness, peace, and the lineage of Judah and David. These are themes that keep repeating.

Isaiah is one prophet who received numerous revelations of a different kingdom coming that would bring about the greatest restoration of all. He saw the wolf dwelling with the lamb, the leopard with the kid, the cow and the bear grazing together, the lion eating straw like the ox, and children playing with vipers.[45] Isaiah told the people,

> Arise, shine; for your light has come, and the glory of the LORD has risen upon you. For behold, darkness will cover the earth, and deep darkness the peoples; but the LORD will rise upon you, and His glory will appear upon you. And nations will come to your light and kings to the brightness of your rising.[46]

Once again, darkness is coming, but the light comes along with the glory of God appearing on His people.

THE REASON FOR THE CROSS

In a way that no one could understand, especially with all the spiritual darkness in the world, God came in a form and at a time that no one was expecting. They wanted a conquering king, like David, to overthrow the reign of the Roman Empire, one of the most powerful empires to ever exist. Yet Isaiah stated, "Behold, the virgin shall be with child, and shall bear a son, and they shall call his name 'Immanuel, which translated means, 'God with Us.'"[47] The "seed of the woman" came to earth, and Mary gave birth to Him in Bethlehem, the city of David. It was a man who disobeyed God and brought all the curses on the world. The only legal way to restore everything back to its original intent would require a man to be completely dependent on God and be obedient to Him in all things.

When Jesus came of age with the qualifications as a priest according to the Law, He walked into the synagogue and read the following passage out of Isaiah:

> "The Spirit of the Lord GOD is upon me, because the LORD has anointed me to bring good news to the afflicted; He has sent me to bind up the brokenhearted, to proclaim liberty to captives, and freedom to prisoners; to proclaim the favorable year of the LORD."[48]

The good news that Jesus shared not only set prisoners free but healed people physically, raised the dead, and brought people into proper relationship with their God. "The favorable year of the Lord" normally refers to the year of Jubilee, where, every fiftieth year, all slaves were set free, all debts were cancelled, and all land was returned to its original owner. However, any year that the Lord shows up in your life can be considered favorable!

After living a life of perfection in submission to the will of the Father and through the anointing of the Holy Spirit, the seed of the woman,

Jesus, had to die in order to bring forth life "after His own kind." The way Jesus had to die came in great detail as well, although one would have to look for it to put the pieces together. This began with His sinless life, because "the Lamb of God who takes away the sin of the world," like the Passover lamb, had to be a male lamb without any blemish that was then sacrificed.[49] According to Leviticus, "the life is in the blood," so the blood of the sacrifice had to be sprinkled in order to bring atonement for sin.[50] Isaiah stated the following concerning the "suffering servant":

> He was despised and forsaken of men, a man of sorrows and acquainted with grief; and like one from whom men hide their face, He was despised and we did not esteem Him. Surely our griefs he Himself bore, and our sorrows He carried; yet we ourselves esteemed Him stricken, smitten of God and afflicted. But He was pierced for our transgressions, He was crushed for our iniquities; the chastening for our well-being fell upon Him, and by his scourging we are healed.[51]

Since a curse was on humanity as well as all creation, Jesus would have to *become* a curse in order to bear the curse. Within Deuteronomy, the Scripture states, "Cursed is every man who hangs on a tree."[52] However, the man would have to be buried that same day, according to that same passage in Deuteronomy.[53] What are the odds that the form of torture and death within the Roman Empire were scourging and crucifixion (hanging on a "tree" in the form of a cross), respectively? How much do you think God values our restoration? God moves with intentionality and fulfills every detail.

After Jesus was crucified, He was placed in a tomb, and like a seed, He was buried that same day in fulfillment of the Scriptures. Thus, the seed of the woman died and was sown in the ground.[54] All of creation and all of history hinges on the event that occurred on the third day when Jesus was raised from the dead as "the last Adam and became a life-giving spirit."[55] Thus, God produced a seed after His own kind that restored eternal life to humanity and took on the curse so that it might be removed from all of creation. When God is in charge of a restoration project, you can be assured that He will do a complete work that includes every minute detail.

The apostle John had a close relationship with the Lord Jesus, which even Peter acknowledged.[56] The theology within the literature of John's writing is awe-inspiring. When it comes to every detail, God had a plan to establish His will and restore all that was lost. When Jesus first appeared on the third day after being raised from the dead, this is what John stated when Jesus appeared to Mary Magdalene: "Jesus said to her, 'Woman, why are you weeping? Whom are you seeking?' *Supposing Him to be the gardener,* she said to Him, 'Sir, if you have carried Him away, tell me where you have laid Him, and I will take Him away.'"[57] Now there is no coincidence in Scripture or in the language used here. Adam was a gardener and was commanded "to tend the garden and to keep it."[58] The first place Jesus appears is in a garden and is called a gardener! So Jesus picked up right where Adam missed it. Where would Jesus pick up in your life in order to reset everything?

THE WHOLE EARTH

So if the small things matter to God, what do you think He has in store for all of creation that is alive? As I already mentioned, the apostle John had a special relationship with the Lord Jesus and wrote his gospel about sixty years after He was resurrected. One of the most-quoted verses by John states, "For God so loved the world, that He gave His only begotten Son, that whoever believes in Him should not perish, but have eternal life."[59] Within this verse, the word for world is κόσμος, *kosmos,* which means "harmonious arrangement, order, government, the whole mass of men alienated from God, the whole circle of earthly goods, all of creation, the entire world system, universe."[60] God so loved the world—the entire world and all of its systems.

Interestingly, a crown of thorns was placed on the head of Jesus by the Roman soldiers.[61] Jesus literally took the curse of the land upon His head. God cared for all of creation, not just humanity. Additionally, the Roman soldiers "cast lots for his clothing," because it was seamless and therefore expensive.[62] The world market system and gambling even came into the jurisdiction of Jesus's crucifixion.

Paul the apostle received a revelation concerning creation. He wrote:

> For the anxious longing of the creation waits eagerly for the revealing of the sons of God. For the creation was subjected to futility, not of its own will, but because of Him who subjected it, in hope that the creation itself also will be set free from its slavery to corruption into the freedom of the glory of the children of God. For we know that the whole creation groans and suffers the pains of childbirth together until now.[63]

The entire earth and everything in it longs to be completely restored. Are the earthquakes and volcanoes "the pains of childbirth" in the earth longing to be renewed and restored the way God designed it? Obviously, created things are not God, but God is working and moving in all of creation. However, Paul linked the sons of God and children of God taking their proper place in the *kosmos* in order to institute the restoration of creation.

ALL PEOPLE MATTER

As alluded to in the definition of *kosmos*, all of the people alienated from God are included in the world system. No matter what prejudice a person may have, God desires all people to have a place in His kingdom and be restored. God wants all of us to fulfill our potential. The apostle Peter understood this when he wrote, "The Lord is not slow about His promise, as some count slowness, but is patient toward you, not wishing for any to perish but for all to come to repentance."[64]

Within the book of Revelation, "every tribe, tongue, people and nation" is seen worshiping in heaven.[65] Jesus purchased all of these different people groups from every nation on the planet with His own blood.[66] The Gospel, or "good news," is meant to be shared with all people around the world. The good news is that restoration is available to all. This includes every aspect of a person—body, soul, and spirit. Furthermore, the restoration includes all aspects of our existence—socially, relationally, and financially.

Peter may have been brief in his letter and in his message, but his point was made very clear. Everything that the Lord wants restored will happen before He returns.[67] This means that there is still a lot of work that must be done. That means that we must be in the restoration business, no matter who we are. This might be one person at a time, one community at a time, or an entire nation at one time. But one thing is for sure: there is no limit to the amount of restoration that God wants to see accomplished.

POINTS TO PONDER

1. What is so significant about a seed, and what seeds do you have that can be moved upon?
2. So, if the small things matter to God, what do you think He has in store for all of creation that is alive?
3. What would your life look like if you lacked nothing at all?
4. How much do you think God values our restoration?
5. Where would Jesus pick up in your life in order to reset everything?

3

THE WIDOW'S WONDER

The person who receives a prophet in the name of a prophet shall receive a prophet's reward.[68]

Timing can be everything, even when it comes to providential timing. Have you ever been telling a story about an individual and that person just happens to walk into the room? This is exactly what happens when Gehazi is recounting the story of a woman who had her son resurrected—literally brought back to life—by the prophet Elisha. Interestingly, we do not even know the name of the woman or her son, but they make history and Scripture nonetheless.

What gets a no-name woman and her son into the Scriptures? It is not just the resurrection of the son but the convergence of several details that could only occur through divine intervention. In conjunction with the convergence, the "restoration of all things" goes beyond what the human mind could ask or imagine.[69] Consider her story and examine if you have any similarities reflected in your life.

MAKING ROOM FOR THE PROPHET

In 2 Kings 4, it is noted that a prominent woman from Shunem noticed that Elisha passed by her house, so she invited him for food.[70] She made a habit of feeding him every time he came by her house.[71] Through these meal times, the Shunamite perceived that Elisha was a "holy man of God."[72] Clearly, something stood out about his character or demeanor that caught her attention. This woman's prominence became apparent since she told her husband to make an "upper chamber with a bed, table, chair, and lampstand."[73]

First, she and her husband had the wealth to add on to their current residence. In the Middle East, a house is normally built to hold only the family, and extra room is truly a luxury. Second, the Shunamite also had the ability to buy furniture and place it in the room, which would only be used by Elisha when he came by and remained at the house during his sojourns. The amount of time that passed between his visits is not given, but we know that Elisha's visits spanned over years.

As the Shunammite woman's story continues to unfold, the detail comes out that her husband was old and they did not have any children.[74] Elisha cared for this woman and her family and asked what he could do for her (them).[75] He had his servant, Gehazi, call her to him so that he could speak with her.[76] Then Elisha made a declaration: "At this season next year, you shall embrace a son."[77] To any woman who has not been able to have a child, this is no small statement.

Even more so, in the ancient Near East, the firstborn son would have been the one to receive the inheritance of the family. If there was no son, the inheritance would go to the nearest relative. Having a son meant that the family name as well as the estate would be carried on in perpetuity, which was an honor. The fact that they had no sons was actually a sign of dishonor, or a lack of blessing, even though this woman was described as "prominent." The declaration of a son by Elisha was a restoration of hope as well as honor.

Honoring the Prophetic Word

Holding on to a prophetic word and honoring that word became crucial for the Shunammite woman. A number of years must have passed, since her son is no longer an infant.[78] This young man went out to the field to see his father but stated that his head was bothering him.[79] A servant carried him to his mother, the Shunammite woman, and she held him until noon when he died.[80] At this point, most people would give up any kind of hope and doubt God even cares about them, their circumstances, or their life. However, something must have been ignited in this Shunammite woman from the prophetic word that the prophet Elisha had delivered.

The Shunammite did not simply bury him and grieve her loss. She had the young man's body placed on the bed in the chamber made for Elisha and requested a donkey so that she could go after this man of God.[81] She embarked on a search and found Elisha at Mount Carmel, and Elisha noticed her from a distance.[82] The prophet inquired if all was well with the Shunammite and her family, because his statement revealed "the LORD had hidden the concern from him."[83] Amazingly, the response of the Shunammite was remarkable, because she stated, "It is well."[84]

Some of us who know the stages of grief might say that she was in complete denial. But this may not be the case here. The declaration of the Shunammite could reveal that a hope had been set ablaze in her due to the word from the prophet. Her actions demonstrated this, because her contemplation might have been on the goodness of God, who is concerned about the conditions of this world. If the Shunammite woman had given up all hope, none of this would have transpired.

Once Elisha learned what truly happened, he sent his servant, Gehazi, ahead of him with his staff, to set it on the young man until he arrived at the Shunammite's house.[85] When Elisha and the Shunammite arrived at the house, the son was not alive, so he went into the room, prayed to the LORD, and acted upon what he heard to restore this young man to life.[86] The Shunammite woman's son came to life once again, and she honored the prophet—but she had already honored the prophetic word continuously with her prophetic actions.[87]

As if this was not enough to endure, the Shunammite had to honor another prophetic word. Elisha told her that a famine was coming on the land for seven years, so she had to "sojourn wherever she could sojourn."[88] Don't you love how accurate that is? On top of having to leave the family inheritance behind, the Shunammite was not even given a hint as to where to go, but she was told she could not remain where she was.

Funded by Enemies

Interestingly, the only thing revealed about the Shunammite's seven-year sojourn was her rough relocation among the Philistines. Like the patriarchs of old, the Shunammite repeated history and dwelt among the Philistines, a seafaring, warrior ethnic group. They worshiped Dagon, which involved detestable practices, including child sacrifice. This was not exactly a dream destination, considering she had a miracle in the form of her son ... twice. The Philistines warred with every other civilization around them, so there is no question that this lady ended up in enemy territory.

The fascinating facets of this come into play, however. As history does repeat itself, the Shunammite and her family survive the famine among the Philistines, just like the patriarchs. Since they survived this, one must ask, "How did they make it?" Since the Shunammite family had no land to work, it is possible that they could have worked the land of a Philistine. In the midst of a famine, was this land not affected? This remains a mystery. The only fact that can be grasped is that the Shunammite family was funded in enemy territory for seven years!

There is a proverb that states, "When a man's ways are pleasing to the Lord, He makes even his enemies to be at peace with him."[89] When any person honors the prophet or the Word of God, they do please the Lord because this demonstrates faith. Not only did the Shunammite come out of Philistine territory funded, she came out with her family, including her son. Trusting and obeying God may not be easy, but obedience is the safest place to be, even in enemy territory.

The Timing of Restoration

Not only did the Shunammite honor the prophetic word, but the servant of Elisha, Gehazi, also honored the prophetic acts as well. In 2 Kings 8, Gehazi was recounting the story to the king of Israel of this woman and her son, along with other stories of what Elisha had done.[90] It just so happened, when Gehazi was talking about the Shunammite and her son, she walked into the king's court with her son to appeal for her house and her field to be restored to her.[91]

Now this turned out to be another miracle, just in the timing. How could the Shunammite have planned to walk in to the king's court just as Gehazi was recounting her story? No earthly figure could have pulled this off. Only divine timing could have made this occur. This was not an instant restoration either. Remember, she and her family had endured seven years in Philistine territory. The miracle occasionally has been wrapped up in the mystery of God working certain details out that our human capacity has no idea how to create or calculate out at precisely the right time. Yet the Shunammite received yet another supernatural breakthrough that revealed even more, and it happened at the hand of God.

TRIPLE RESTORATION

Entering the court of a king or a ruler is not an easy task. Protocol is involved. Security is involved. Bookkeeping is involved. Due to my placing and position in the capital of Wyoming as the highest-ranking chaplain within the Wyoming Air Guard, I have been in the Wyoming governor's office several times, so I know that a person does not just wander up to the door and come in. All of the different customs and courtesies, along with the order of business, happen when they happen. So let us get back to the Shunammite family.

When the Shunammite came before the king, he asked her of the story, and she "related it to him."[92] After hearing the story, the king appointed an officer to restore all that was hers.[93] The family received their land as well as their house back to them. But there is more to this story as well. The king stated, "Restore all that was hers and all the produce of the field from the day that she left the land even until now."[94] As a reminder, there had been a famine in the land for seven years. So how did this land have produce?

In their absence, the land supernaturally produced for seven years. So the Shunammite not only received the house and land, she also received seven years' worth of income from the produce of the land in the midst of a famine. Once again, only the hand of God could have made this happen. When God brought about restoration, He miraculously produced more life and bounty than the Shunammite could have ever conceived in her life.

IT CAN HAPPEN TO YOU

When it comes to applying a biblical narrative to our own lives, we must remember that this is Scripture, and God does not lie or change.[95] Additionally, "God is no respecter of persons."[96] The miracles, favor, and restoration that can happen to one person can potentially manifest in the lives of others. The Scriptures contain numerous accounts of various people receiving their lives and livelihood back in every way or declaring that God will ultimately bring about "the restoration of all things."[97]

What would *everything being restored to your life* look like? If this might be too broad of a question, consider aspects of the Shunammite's story in your life. If your longing for children has not been answered yet, keep contending. If you have suffered loss of lands or a family inheritance, do not give up hope. The events that were told in just one chapter unfolded over years. Perhaps some action must happen to demonstrate your faith. As one scribe declared, "Through faith and patience, we inherit the promises."[98] This particular scribe truly was inspired, because patience must be coupled with faith. Some people wait a lifetime to see the restoration that they are longing for.

Anything that is worth restoring is also worth the wait. Not only is the restoration worth the wait, it is worth the price. Do not think any detail too small, and do not consider any obstacle too big. For example, let's revisit my 1965 Barracuda from chapter 1, with thirteen-inch rims and five-lug nuts and bolts. Do you have any idea how hard those were to come by twenty-five years after the car was produced? I went to scrapyards throughout North Carolina searching for one. By the grace of God, the one found in the trunk of another scrapped Barracuda was not only an exact match; it was not warped or rusted, since it had been in the trunk. That's a big obstacle *and* a small detail that God took care of! Pursue the restoration. The outcome God has in mind is truly worth it all.

POINTS TO PONDER

1. What would "everything being restored to your life" look like? Take a sheet of paper—or better yet, a journal—and write them down.
2. What is your greatest longing?
3. What stood out to you about the Shunammite woman's story that relates to your life?
4. Do you remember a time in your life when everything lined up in a remarkable way?

4

A Tale of Friends and the Convergence of Kings

Rejoice with those who rejoice and weep with those who weep.[99]

It is one thing to have a bad day, but does it have to include all of your friends and family too? When I was in college, I was roommates with my brother, Mike, and a Mexican American named Brandon. We all had a mutual friend named John, another Mexican American, who appreciated music and was great at building custom sound systems for cars. We could hear John's car coming down to our townhouse from three blocks away due to the thump of his bass.

Near the end of our spring term, we had been up studying, but we were also enjoying one another's company. John was invited to stay at our place that night so he would not have to go out in the cold. In Laramie, Wyoming, it was still plenty cold, even at the end of April. The following morning, we told John we would see him later, since he was going to help install some speakers in a car.

We did not think much about it, but John did not make it back to our townhouse that evening. The news was released that some guy had walked up to a student and shot him six times. The student was still alive when he was brought to the hospital by paramedics, but there was too much trauma created by the six bullets hitting vital organs. To our dismay, we found out that it was John who had been shot and later died. We did not know that the previous night would be his last on this earth as we knew it. Bewildered, none of us could understand why such a kind, friendly guy, our great friend, would be taken away so suddenly.

We are not the only people who have encountered grief and loss on this kind of scale (see my first book, *The Pathological Grieving of America: Overcoming Grief on a Personal, Corporate and National Scale*).[100] There is no question that grief and loss leave an impression for a lifetime. But what happens when God gets involved in our narrative?

DAVID AND HIS FRIENDS AT ZIKLAG

Before David became king of Israel, he had to flee his own country and had a band of friends who had come around him and formed a community. The narrative of David within 1 and 2 Samuel and his own writings in the form of psalms enable us to grasp how tragedy, triumph, friendship, failure, pain, and repentance come together in a person's life. In the midst of all of these aspects of life, God is intimately involved and knows even the hidden details.

At this point within the story, David was actually living among the enemies of Israel, the Philistines, and even had favor with one of the lords.[101] He had been given a city among them that was named Ziklag, which means "winding."[102] The reference, according to Jewish and Christian interpretation of Scripture, can be literal, figurative, or hidden, often referred to as a "mystery." Perhaps roads or terrain caused a winding in the area. A winding stream could have been close by. Or from me with my Wyoming humor, David just found himself *winding* up right in this location due to a number of circumstances.

We do know David and his men had taken residence in Ziklag for a year and four months, so they had been there long enough to make this their home and hometown.[103] When they came close to home after being sent away by the Philistines three days earlier, they saw smoke rising from the city.[104] After seeing that everything was taken, David and his men "wept until there was no strength in them to weep."[105] The men's grief had turned to anger that became channeled like lightning right toward David, because the men spoke of stoning him.[106] However, in the midst of all of this, "David strengthened himself in the LORD his God."[107] We do not know if that means David grabbed a harp and started worshipping the Lord, proclaimed God's goodness, or sat in his burnt house in solitude, remembering all the times God had delivered him.

The next thing David did was ask Abiathar the priest (whose name means "my Father is plenty or great")[108] to bring the ephod, which was their physical representation of God in their midst.[109] Then David inquired of the LORD as to what he and his men should do. The LORD responded, "Pursue, for you shall surely overtake them and you shall surely rescue all."[110] David did not just assume he could pursue this army and fight them, although any one of us would be willing to do whatever it takes to save our family. But at the LORD's declaration, David knew this was the right thing to do at this time. The declaration also proclaimed that they would rescue all! God's heart was for restoration of everything, not just punishing the attackers.

Given a proclamation and a plan, David and his six hundred men pursued the Amalekite horde, but two hundred men were too tired to cross the brook Besor, so they stayed behind.[111] So David and his other four hundred men kept pursuing and providentially found an Egyptian slave who was left behind due to an illness.[112] David made a bargain with the Egyptian not to kill him or turn him over to his former master if he would lead them to the enemy's camp.[113] When they came to the camp and saw them "drinking and dancing because of all the great spoil they had taken from the land, David and his men slaughtered them from the twilight until the evening of the next day."[114] Now remember, before they arrived here, two hundred men were so exhausted they had to stay behind. Now David and these four hundred men had the strength to fight through the night and into the next day until evening!

As the LORD had declared, "David recovered all and nothing of theirs was missing, whether small or great, sons or daughters, spoil, or anything that they had taken for themselves."[115] Additionally, "they captured all the sheep and the cattle which the people drove ahead of the livestock."[116] So not only did they recover everything that they had lost, they gained a surplus that went above and beyond their own possessions.

ALL RECEIVE THE RESTORATION AND REWARD

When David returned to the brook Besor, where the other two hundred men were, another interesting turn of events occurred. We do not know how many of the four hundred men said this, but they are referred to as "wicked and worthless," who stated, "Because they did not go with us, we will not give them any of the spoil we have recovered, except to every man, his wife and his children, that they may lead them away and depart."[117] So not only were they not going to share the reward with the other two hundred, they were going to dismiss them and not allow them to continue dwelling with them.

Is this not interesting? First, the "wicked and worthless" fought for over twenty-four hours to recapture all that was lost. So they actually did put their blood, sweat, and tears into this. So what happened in their hearts on the way back to the other two hundred men that made them not only want to keep the reward from the two hundred but also not want to have any more relationship with them?

Here is where David started acting like a king. He stated:

> You must not do so, my brothers, with what the LORD has given us, who has kept us and delivered into our hand the band that came against us. And who will listen to you in this matter? For as his share is who goes down to the battle, so shall his share be who stays by the baggage; they shall share alike.[118]

First, David started reconciling the men with one another by calling them *brothers*. Second, he established a principle that transcended the normal way of thinking to show that all have equal value to God, and all have an important part to play. In the future, perhaps some of those four hundred men would be too tired to go out and fight. In this way, David took away any shame from the two hundred men who stayed behind, demonstrating they still had significance. David even went beyond his own men and sent spoils to the cities of Judah around him, including the city of Hebron. Incidentally, this name means "friendship or joining," and this is where David was first crowned king.

In our current Christian circles, I have observed some people being jealous of others who have had a major breakthrough. Like David, we should not see this as "*they* win" but as "*we* win." If we can start sharing in one another's victories and rejoice over them rather than become jealous of them, we will see even more victories come exponentially. Every single person has significance, and we must remember this.

Kept from the Wrong Fight

One might ask, "Why did all of this happen?" Any time a person undergoes a tragedy or loss, bargaining can set in, where these kinds of questions are asked. From Scripture, the reason is given in the midst of the literature. Prior to Ziklag being overrun and burned with fire by the Amalekites, David (along with his men, by default) had been willing to go fight alongside the Philistines. They were actually going to fight *against* Israel.

Had David been involved in this fight, he would have lost his credibility with his men and come into disfavor with God. Beforehand, God had delivered King Saul into his hands twice, where he literally could have killed him.[119] Yet David understood a principle, stating, "Do not destroy him, for who can stretch out his and against the LORD's anointed and be without guilt?"[120] All of his men would have remembered David making this statement.

At the end of 1 Samuel, just following David's battle with the Amalekites, the Philistines engaged with King Saul and killed him and all of his sons. Instead of the guilt being on David or his men, it fell on the Philistines. Since David did not get news of the death of King Saul and his sons until after this fight, they must have been occupied with winning their own battle, recovering all of their family and possessions, and rebuilding their houses.

In all things, God works out the most good that is possible. Sometimes, any one of us can end up in a trial or struggle that we do not understand why it happened at that time. Can you look back on a time when you were dealing with a personal struggle that actually kept you out of a much greater disaster? After I became a Christian, my car blew the engine and kept me from going into business. This incident tuned me in to hear the voice of God calling me to something different than business.

David in the Wrong Place at the Wrong Time

We revisit David again in 2 Samuel 11 after some time has passed, when he is now king in Jerusalem. At this point though, he *should* have been involved in a fight but stayed back at his home.[121] If only King David had been in his nation's own campaign, we would not read about the demise of a man's character. We read at this point that King David climbed up on his roof and saw a woman bathing.[122] First, he already had *wives*, not just *a wife*, so why look at another woman? After seeing her, though, he inquired of her and had messengers go get her. She was Bathsheba, married to one of his mighty men, Uriah the Hittite.[123] After their encounter, she became pregnant.[124]

If only the adultery was the end of the depravity. King David decided to try to cover his tracks by inviting Uriah the Hittite back to the city from the front lines so he could be with his wife. However, Uriah the Hittite proved to be of a more noble character than King David and refused to do anything that the men at war could not do.[125] Now this placed David in an even bigger dilemma, because he was not able to disguise his sin.

When King David sent Uriah back to the front lines, the very place where he should have been himself, he had Uriah deliver his own death sentence to Joab, stating, "Place Uriah in the front line of the fiercest battle and withdraw from him so that he may be struck down and die."[126] What makes this even more heinous is that Uriah the Hittite was listed as one of King David's "mighty thirty," which indicated that he had been with David for a while and was one of his best friends, which also could explain the close living quarters in Jerusalem.[127] So in the end, King David lusted, committed adultery, conspired about it, betrayed one of his trusted companions, and had him murdered. King David's one decent act involved taking Bathsheba as his wife after she mourned the loss of her husband.

King David would have gotten away with this, but there is a God who sees everything, and He was not pleased! On the contrary, when a prophet of God was sent to speak with someone one-on-one, this usually meant that the person was about to have a divine confrontation. So God sends Nathan the prophet to King David, and he plays "Columbo" and does not tell him directly that he knows what the king did. Nathan tells a parable to King David, and his response to the story is that the man who acted in such a way should die![128] To King David's surprise, Nathan responds, "You are the man!"[129] Then he proceeds to lay out all of the details of what King David did and pronounces the judgment of God against him.[130]

However, King David unlocked three keys following his divine confrontation. First, he did not do the Christian form of BS, blame-shifting, but confessed, "I have sinned against the LORD."[131] He truly repented. His predecessor, King Saul, set the example of blaming everything and everyone else for his sin and would never own it. Perhaps this is where God's saying came true, that He was going to choose "a man according to his heart."[132]

The second key that King David unlocked was humbling himself with prayer and fasting, even after hearing the judgment against him and his unborn child. Even though the first child conceived with Bathsheba died, King David used a third key to restore his relationship with the LORD. He still "cleaned himself, changed his clothes, and went into the house of the LORD and worshipped."[133] In the midst of all of this, do you think this is where he wrote Psalm 51? Take a look:

> For the choir director, A Psalm of David,
> when Nathan the prophet came to him,
> after he had gone into Bathsheba.
> Be gracious to me, O God, according
> to Your lovingkindness;
> According to the greatness of Thy
> compassion blot out my transgressions.
> Wash me thoroughly from my iniquity
> and cleanse me from my sin.
> For I know my transgressions, and
> my sin is ever before me.

Against Thee, Thee only, I have sinned
and done what is evil in Thy sight,
So that Thou art justified when Thou dost
speak and blameless when Thou dost judge.
Behold, I was brought forth in iniquity,
and in sin my mother conceived me.
Behold, Thou dost desire truth in the
innermost being,
And in the hidden part Thou wilt
make me know wisdom.
Purify me with hyssop, and I shall be clean;
wash me, and I shall be whiter than snow.
Make me to hear joy and gladness, let the
bones which Thou have broken rejoice.
Hide Thy face from my sins and
blot out all my iniquities.
Create in me a clean heart, O God, and
renew a steadfast spirit within me.
Do not cast me away from Thy presence and
do not take Thy Holy Spirit from me.
Restore to me the joy of Thy salvation
and sustain me with a willing spirit.
Then I will teach transgressors Thy ways,
and sinners will be converted to Thee.
Deliver me from bloodguiltiness, O
God, Thou God of my salvation;
then my tongue will joyfully sing of
Thy righteousness.
O Lord, open my lips, that my mouth
may declare Thy praise.
For Thou dost not delight in sacrifice,
otherwise I would give it;
Thou art not pleased with burnt offering.
The sacrifices of God are a broken spirit;
A broken and a contrite heart, O
God, Thou wilt not despise.

By Thy favor do good to Zion; build
the walls of Jerusalem.
Then Thou wilt delight in righteous sacrifices,
In burnt offering and whole burnt offering;
Then young bulls will be offered on Thine altar.[134]

Following this, two new signs occurred in the form of circumstances. First, David and Bathsheba had another child. This son they named "Solomon," but "Jedidiah" was the name given him by the LORD through the prophet Nathan, meaning "Beloved of the LORD."[135] Second, King David did go out to finish the war. He received the spoil in the form of the king's crown placed on his head that weighed one talent of gold with a precious stone.[136] Keep in mind, a talent is seventy-five pounds! I believe these were both signs to King David that, according to his psalm, his restoration had already begun.

THE LOSS OF A KINGDOM AND TWO SONS

Even though God did forgive King David's sin, the judgment that Nathan proclaimed came to pass. Here lies another lesson: sin has consequences. All of this occurred after David's adultery with Bathsheba. Some consequences are more severe than others. Even though God pronounced forgiveness over David's sin, David opened up a gate of hell into his family and into his kingdom. There is a lesson here for all of us.

Absalom had taken vengeance for the rape of his sister and killed his half-brother Amnon.[137] In a way, just by the numbers, it seems as if the gate of hell brought in things that were ten times worse, because Absalom stole the kingdom from his father and set up a tent on the roof of the palace and had relations with ten of his father's concubines.[138] This violated God's law in a number of ways, but to the person who loses character, loses their fear of God, and lacks holiness, there is no limit to the depravity any person can enter. If any person has a temptation that seems overbearing, maybe the question should be, what are the consequences if this route is pursued? If King David had been given a glimpse of what would happen to his family and his kingdom, odds are he would have thought twice, at the least.

DAVID IS FULLY RESTORED

So as a recap, David had been anointed king. Then after he became king, he had failures, from taking Uriah's wife to taking a census of the Israelites. David's disobedience and dysfunction opened gateways to atrocities in his life. Absalom, David's son, killed his half-brother Amnon, who had raped Absalom's sister Tamar. David pardoned Absalom but did not restore his relationship with him. In turn, Absalom schemed a way of stealing David's attention. David lost the capital and the kingdom to his own son, Absalom. David gained the kingdom back but at the loss of Absalom through a civil war. Though it cost David the lives of two sons, Amnon and Absalom, a disgraced daughter, a lost kingdom, and lost concubines, he was restored back to the kingdom of Israel as the king.

God restored David after committing lust, adultery, betrayal, conspiracy, and murder. Who are we to limit the restoration power of God? Keep in mind, also, this was even before the cross of Christ! How much more reason should we have, as Christians, when it comes to our commitment to restoration? In no way should we ever limit the cross of Christ in being able to save, deliver, heal, and restore any person.

Beyond King David's restoration as king, his own lineage is established as the one the Messiah came through, which happened to be through Solomon, David and Bathsheba's son. This is one of the greatest signs of true mercy, grace, and complete restoration, even to Bathsheba. When it comes to God's mercy, grace, and restoration, He is limitless in what He is willing and able to do.

POINTS TO PONDER

1. Can you look back on a time when you were dealing with a personal struggle that actually kept you out of a much greater disaster?
2. Do you strengthen yourself in the LORD when you face a trial or struggle? If this is not your first response, how do you respond?
3. Have you inquired of the LORD what His direction is for you at this time in your life?
4. Every single person has significance, and we must remember this.
5. If King David were alive today, would he have been allowed to be restored to his original role and sphere of authority?

5

THE SPIRITUAL THING TO DO

2 Cor 13:11a Finally Brothers, rejoice. Aim for Restoration.[139]

Given the number of times restoration is observed in the Bible, I keep asking, "Why do we not see this in the body of Christ more often?" If this is what we as Christians are supposed to aim for, then we must pursue this at a much greater level. We should be aiming for restoration.

There is no question that the world loves restoration. There are a number of episodes and shows with people restoring houses, classic cars, and antiques. Yet King David, as a psalmist, understood God to be a restorer. In one of the most universally recognized psalms, David stated, "He restores my soul."[140] I hope that the church as well as modern culture will realize that the restoration of people is more valuable than any material object. According to numerous stories in Scripture, this truth becomes reality. Rather than a rarity, this reality will manifest in the church as the kingdom of God is extended.

Restoration, to Paul the apostle, was the pinnacle of Christian love in action, according to his letter written to the Galatians. He stated, "Brethren, even if anyone is caught in any trespass, you who are spiritual, restore such a one in a spirit of gentleness; each one looking to yourself, so that you too will not be tempted. Bear one another's burdens, and thereby fulfill the law of Christ."[141] Clearly, no one is exempt from being restored, no matter how great the sin is perceived to be. When we think of "any person committing any trespass," we can create the application being acceptable to "pardonable" matters, such as stealing someone's parking space at church. However, God's perspective encompasses all.

Whether it is Greek or English, *any* means "any." This includes the murderer, child molester, rapist, or any other mortal sin one can conceive. King David betrayed, committed adultery, murdered, and lied to cover it up, and God *still* restored him! This was before the cross. And after the cross, no limits exist for restoration. There is a reason that David was inspired to write and sing songs on restoration.

When it comes to restoration, the concept is simple and applicable. The practice of restoration is rare. In the military, as well as in many other realms today, a goal is measured by being SMART: specific, measurable, attainable, recordable, and time-specific. When it comes to practicing restoration, the ability to create a SMART goal seems vague. How do we measure someone's repentance? How do we measure the person's longevity or process of restoration? Is the person able to obtain the same position they held before their failure? These types of questions shall be considered, but consider how far some people have fallen in the past.

THE FALL

If we were to go back in time just a little, there is the case of Jim Jones leading a group of people to form their own community in Guyana. Ultimately, he convinced all of them to commit suicide by drinking poison together.[142] Even though I was just born when this happened, I have heard this story repeated a number of times. The Jim Jones case tainted the perception of the body of Christ. This one case seemed to give the media the thrill of exposing any man of God who had an ethical or moral failure. Failures within the fold have continued to be highlighted, so how can the body of Christ change the narrative? Due to the tragic ending of this story, we do not know if a restoration process could have been possible with Jim Jones or with his group of followers. But in my mind, there is one narrative that sets the tone for restoration.

My father went through his own crucible in 1977, admitting to a drinking problem that had been present since taking his first drink in high school. Dad had worked for J.C. Penney since before he graduated high school and was the manager of a store in Hettinger, North Dakota. Amazingly, the company did not fire him but was willing to pay him while he went through his rehabilitation—*and* pay for the rehab on top of that. He spent six months at the Heartview Clinic in Mandan, North Dakota. Upon completion of his rehab program, he was restored as the manager of the same store.

Something happened to my dad while he was in treatment. After he returned home, he watched the PTL Club with Jim Bakker and was moved to the point of tears. Thanks to my dad, I knew what the PTL Club was, and it was not just because of the puppet show. My father had undergone another transformation while he was at the Heartview Clinic, which is something I would not personally understand for another fifteen years.

By the late 1980s, the culture was not just known for unique hair, clothing styles, or the best music ever. The media ensured that any person within ministry or representing God who failed became exposed as much as possible. A number of different denominations and movements throughout the body of Christ had prominent ministers or priests who were publicly exposed. Scripture did say that "judgment would begin at the household of God," but God or the church should be the one to do the judging or discipline, respectively.[143]

In my own memory, the collapse of PTL and Rev. Jim Bakker were at the forefront. Since I was not walking with God at this time, I cannot personally speak to the reaction or actions of the body of Christ other than what I researched or observed. I had an opportunity to visit the Heritage USA campus prior to its closing. A good friend of mine started college in Rock Hill, South Carolina, and I would go there to visit him when I had a long weekend while I was stationed at Ft. Bragg, North Carolina.

The secular arena has not cared much for Scripture, especially used in context or with the right motives. Some big names were not just exposed in the 1980s but completely taken down, and the media gloated in this. Like flies on a dead carcass, the media would swarm the man, the ministry, or both, for years. Another principal player has always worked behind the scenes. Paul referred to this as the "prince of the power of the air."[144] Since the fall, the truth has been distorted, manipulated, or hidden.

In this information age, there is no coincidence that broadcasting is "on the air." Specifically, this Ephesians verse states that the "children of disobedience" fall under this power. Nearly the entire mountain of media remains outside Christian circles. Therefore, a Christian perspective or gospel truth has not been given a priority. This must be understood, especially in Rev. Bakker's case, along with the moral failures exposed during this same time frame.

My perspective as a child witnessing my father being restored informed my worldview into adulthood. In my natural mind, I wondered, *How can a corporation see the value in treating and restoring a manager like my dad, but treating and restoring a minister seems inconceivable to the church and to the secular arena?* As I stated, I was not walking with Christ at this time, and it was a thought that bewildered me to observe.

Even in the military, a member could be restored after a huge failure if he or she were willing to go through some discipline and a process. There was even a soldier we nicknamed "Velcro" in the 1980s because of being disciplined and losing rank so many times. In the 1980s, rank was sewn on, so we thought this would have made life easier for him! As he responded to a restoration process, Velcro was able to obtain his rank back. So if corporate America and the military can perceive the value of restoring people, what are the odds of this being realized within the body of Christ?

PRISON

Not the first choice for anyone, prison has become the answer to a lot of the cases in our society. The original intent of holding someone was to "punish the offender as well as allow personal reform," or to become *penitent*, which is where the word *penitentiary* came from.[145] From a Judeo-Christian perspective, people are not considered inherently good and need a divine intervention to transform them.[146] Hence, the penitentiary gave people an opportunity to have a divine encounter and experience a transformation within the soul.

The founders of the prison system within the USA were the Quakers.[147] Once good behavior was observed, the offender could be released. If the modern prison changed behavior, the prison system would not be overflowing or be established as a for-profit business. Therefore, if anyone comes out of this system and not only integrates back into society but is restored, God must have implemented a transformation that is not visible on the surface.

Within Scripture, this can be seen a number of times, when it was not necessarily the prisoner who did something to get locked up, but the circumstances framed the person. Joseph is a classic example. He actually had integrity and would not have relations with his master's wife.[148] However, she caught Joseph in the house alone and framed him because he would not touch her. Even though Potiphar, Joseph's master, burned with anger, he probably had an idea that his own wife tried to initiate something; otherwise the accusation as a slave-rapist would not have kept Joseph alive.[149] Joseph would have been executed in a way to set the example for every other slave in Egypt!

Joseph did not anticipate a transition from a slave to a prisoner, but God was still with him, even in the midst of the prison.[150] As Paul Harvey would say, if we knew the rest of the story, we would not have believed that the final outcome would result in Joseph being made the second-highest-ranking official in all of the Egyptian Empire. Not everyone goes straight from prison into a palace. The transformation within Joseph must have been substantial enough that Pharaoh noticed something unique about his character. God also knows the heart and can providentially place someone where they need to be.

Considering the number of offenses that do not land people in prison, the circumstances surrounding Jim Bakker's case leave one in bewilderment. Providentially, Jamie Buckingham published an article titled "Praying for the Forgotten," in which he compared the sentence of Rev. Bakker to notable criminals who were given much less.[151] Following this article, Jim received a visit from Dr. Chuck Colson, who had established a prison ministry after his own ordeal and release.[152] Clearly, God was at work behind the scenes while He was giving Rev. Bakker tangible evidence of His care for him. Notably, a Harvard law professor named Alan Dershowitz looked into Rev. Bakker's case and saw a puzzle that needed to be solved because the severity of the punishment did not fit the accusation.[153] An appeal process had begun, but it did not have immediate traction.

Like Joseph, someone noticed him, but he still remained in prison for years. Joseph had interpreted the dreams of the baker and cupbearer correctly, but the cupbearer, despite his promise to mention Joseph before

Pharaoh, did not mention him until Pharaoh had two disturbing dreams more than two years later.[154] In Rev. Bakker's case, before his appeal took hold, it would seem like a great country song. Jim's wife left him for his best friend, and his son Jamie was the one to confirm it to him.[155] As with many people facing prison, Rev. Bakker battled depression, which is like hitting a tar foe that just covers and engulfs the person that fights with it.[156]

RELEASE

Getting released from a physical prison is a process that takes time, depending on the sentence and the result of the parole hearing. Getting released from a prison involving our own beliefs, worldview, or labels placed on us from others over a lifetime is where the painstaking work occurs. Only God knows the inward journey that a person has taken, because He initiated the transformation along with the release in the first place. The only aspect a person may observe is the fruit of the release.

The metaphor within Malachi creates a vivid video of release: "But for you who fear My name, the sun of righteousness will rise with healing in its wings; and you will go forth and skip about like calves from the stall."[157] Coming from rural country in Wyoming and the Dakotas, I have seen a calf come out of that stall leaping around and jumping! Within this verse, a declaration of release exists for those who fear His name.[158] This type of fear is not the typical scary kind but one that shows reverence. Reverence is defined as "honor or respect felt or shown; deference, especially: profound adoring, awed respect."[159]

This reverence and respect is followed by the "sun of righteousness rising with healing in its wings."[160] Now this is another metaphor that paints an unusual picture. The sun represents light and life, where everything is visible and flourishing. Righteousness in a context of faith implicates a "right standing with God or justice."[161] Therefore, within the release, a reset has occurred, and God is aware of what has happened.

RESTORATION

When it comes to the restoration of a person, one might question the process or the timing of this. Like restoring a rare car, the process can be tedious, with huge gaps of time spent waiting for the right piece to be manufactured or found. When it comes to a person being restored, God is the one who is picking up the pieces and is being meticulous with how everything comes together so that complete wholeness is the result. Remember my friend's definition of *shalom*? "Nothing missing, nothing broken."[162] Other than God, no one has a concrete idea of what the result of restoration should be, along with the timing. However, through time, any person can recognize wholeness within a person's life.

While in prison, Rev. Bakker wondered if, "through some miracle, [he] might be released from prison and restored to Christian ministry."[163] Rev. Bakker added, "My correspondents had much more faith than I had."[164] Prayers initiated the incubation and ignited the process for restoration. Faith and prayer remain keys to practically everything in the Christian faith, including restoration. More importantly, God has designed the body of Christ to be restorers. The healing and restoration cannot be done in a vacuum; it requires others to come alongside the person in order to give edification, exhortation, and comfort.

Amazingly, restoration started for Rev. Bakker the same moment as all the accusations. Due to limited human capacity, the work that God had begun was not perceived by many people, both inside and outside the church. However, all of that changed when Rev. Billy Graham showed up at the prison where Rev. Bakker was being confined.[165] If anything could be a sign that God is working in your life, a personal visit from Billy Graham would certainly be it! After being voted one of the "most influential men in the world," Rev. Graham showed up to visit with Rev. Bakker and have a time of prayer with him. Even Jim was shocked at the visitation.[166] How would you feel if the most influential minister of the time came and visited you?

After losing everything, including his wife, Rev. Bakker had a number of circumstances to overcome. He had pride swallowed up and consumed with humility, which shocked the media that was expecting something else. Even by his book title, Jim stated, "I was wrong."[167] Humility has a way of attracting the grace and mercy of God toward us. His day of liberty, July 1, 1994, was like a country song that was beginning to play in reverse.

Rev. Bakker has been entrusted with insight and perspective that the body of Christ has needed. God restored him to ministry and to television through his program *The Jim Bakker Show*. Now, if you read Jim Bakker's book, you will observe that his ordeal and process of restoration took years. He did not launch this show the day after he came out of prison. He did not get remarried right away either, but it is written, "He who finds a wife finds a good thing and obtains favor from the LORD."[168] Jim eventually married Lori Beth Graham, and they have shared a remarkable story on the goodness of God and the process of restoration. Additionally, they have been at the forefront of getting people ready for the days ahead with messages in due season and products to sustain the individual, family, and community.

POINTS TO PONDER

1. How can the body of Christ change the narrative on restoration?
2. Who have you thought was beyond restoration?
3. How would a restoration process or ministry change the perception of your church?
4. How would you feel if the most influential minister of the time came and visited you?
5. What steps or goals would you implement to oversee a restoration process?

6

THE PARADOX OF RESTORATION

We cannot always bloom where we are planted. Sometimes, we need to be transplanted where the conditions are favorable for growth.

With the complicated nature of restoration within the body of Christ, if a person is restored and brought back into the fold or into their function in ministry, it normally does not happen in the same place or even in the same movement or denomination. If restoration is the heartbeat of God throughout much of Scripture, how can this be? Therefore, this paradox exists, which also forms the question, "Why is this?" The term *paradox* means "a statement or proposition that seems self-contradictory or absurd but in reality expresses a possible truth;" or another definition: "a self-contradictory and false proposition."[169] I want to focus on this latter definition here.

THE BIBLICAL MODEL

According to numerous stories in Scripture, people are clearly more valued and important to restore than any material object. I focused earlier on King David being restored because the guy lusted, committed adultery, betrayed his friend, conspired against his friend, and murdered him and still was restored as king, even before Christ died on the cross! As I mentioned in quoting the passage from Galatians 6 in the last chapter, the spiritual thing to do is to restore the person caught in *any* trespass.[170] Reverend Bakker was restored to where God had placed him before, but it was not with the same ministry or even in the same city. Here is where the paradox is. Let us consider a biblical case from both the Hebrew and Greek references. Now that we have the redemption of all humanity in mind, the restoration of one of our brothers or sisters in Christ is always the goal.

NOT ALL IN THE FAMILY

When it comes to Joseph, I am sure every family member can relate to having a dreamer in the family. However some families place the "diss" in dysfunctional much more than others. Joseph did not help matters when he boasted about his dreams to his family.[171] Joseph was certainly a unique individual, but he "brought back a bad report" about his brothers that did not help their relationship at all.[172] To add insult to injury, Jacob, now called Israel, "loved Joseph more than all his sons and gave him a vari-colored tunic."[173] By the time Joseph bragged about his dreams where he saw all of his family bowing down to him, the tipping point had been reached for the brothers. Now, there is never an excuse for sinful behavior, but the passage painted a very clear picture of Joseph's brothers being pushed too far.

SOLD OUT

When Joseph's brothers were out in the field tending the sheep, Joseph was given the task to go check on them.[174] If Israel had known how much Joseph's brothers had come to despise him, he would not have sent him. Anyone who enjoys a good narrative can anticipate what is about to happen. Once again, the theology is revealed in the literature. Joseph manages to find his brothers but has no idea that they are actually plotting to kill him—all except for the oldest son, Reuben, who has a conscience at this point and rescues Joseph from being killed.[175] Now take note of what Reuben's intent was: "that he might rescue him out of their hands, to *restore* him to his father."[176] Restoration was at the heart of what Reuben wanted to achieve.

When one person has a heart for restoration but others in the family or community do not, things can be derailed in a hurry! Reuben had left the scene with a plan to rescue Joseph, only to come back and find out his brothers had not killed Joseph but sold him into slavery to some Ishmaelites.[177] At this point, Reuben had no way of restoring Joseph back to his father. As the firstborn, he took responsibility for this ordeal, but his brothers covered up the sale by taking Joseph's tunic and smearing it with blood.[178] In this way, they gave their father the impression that he had been attacked by a predator.[179] In reality, the Ishmaelites sold Joseph in Egypt to Pharaoh's officer, Potiphar.[180]

RELOCATION LEADS TO RESTORATION

Only God could have set Joseph up for success. Potiphar also happened to be the captain of Pharaoh's bodyguard.[181] Joseph could have been sold to someone much less prestigious, but proximity is power. Additionally, Joseph had favor from God in the area of administration so that all that he handled prospered.[182] Potiphar became blessed because of Joseph.[183] Joseph did bloom where he was planted, but he was placed in new potting soil.

All went well with Joseph, considering he was a slave. Perhaps Potiphar had other plans for Joseph that would have made him excel and be in the presence of Pharaoh, but we do not know how this scenario could have played out over time. Potiphar's wife gazed on Joseph and wanted ownership of him in other ways, but he would not dishonor God or his master.[184] When Joseph had his guard down, Potiphar's wife cornered him and grabbed his garment, but he fled to the outside of the house.[185] She then framed Joseph to make it look like his fault.[186]

If a reader did not know the storyline, they would be surprised that Joseph was not executed after the trial he endured. We do know that Potiphar did send him to prison, but Joseph received favor from the chief jailer.[187] Due to this favor, Joseph was given charge over all the prisoners and administration.[188] Therefore, Joseph gained the opportunity to interact with all the prisoners and hear what they experienced.

IT TAKES A DREAMER TO RESTORE A DREAMER

While caring for the prisoners and the jail, Joseph noticed that two other prisoners possessed a dejected countenance.[189] Considering this was prison more than three thousand years ago, their faces must have looked much worse than everyone else's. As a good steward, Joseph's attention was drawn to their faces. After hearing that both the cupbearer and the baker had dreams they could not interpret, Joseph asked them both to recount their dreams to him.[190]

The cupbearer presented his dream to Joseph first. When Joseph heard the dream, he gave the interpretation. Joseph told the cupbearer that he would be restored to Pharaoh's service in three days.[191] Notice that Joseph interpreted a dream that dealt with restoration. Have you ever heard someone else's dream and thought it might apply to you? After hearing a favorable interpretation about restoration, the baker shared his dream.[192] Unfortunately, the baker's dream did not have the same interpretation. Joseph stated that the chief baker would have his head removed and his body hanged—and that was exactly what happened.[193] No doubt, the cupbearer kept his best behavior before Pharaoh. He did not want to lose his head. But the cupbearer was restored with a purpose. He was a sign to Joseph and a messenger to Pharaoh.

Being in the pit of despair could be a prison in itself. Joseph possibly hoped that this servant to Pharaoh would have shared about his abilities within a week or two. Have you ever felt like things were going to turn around on a certain time line, but they did not? The cupbearer forgot about Joseph's dream interpretation until Pharaoh had two dreams that disturbed him greatly … two years later.[194] Pharaoh recounted his dreams to the magicians, but they could not interpret them.[195] After the cupbearer mentioned that Joseph could interpret dreams accurately, Pharaoh called him to his court so he could recount his dreams to him.[196] Prior to hearing Pharaoh's dreams, Joseph honored God, acknowledging that He was the one who could give a "favorable answer."[197] God had done such a work in Joseph's heart he knew God was at work to demonstrate His glory.

Joseph told Pharaoh God was telling him what He was about to do.[198] He also told Pharaoh that the "repeating of dreams twice meant that the matter was determined by God, and God will quickly bring it about."[199] Paul the apostle also acknowledged that every *rhema*—the transliteration of the Greek word for "a God-inspired message"—is established by the testimony of two or three witnesses.[200] Remember, Joseph also received two different dreams in the same night. Do you think that Joseph is just speaking to Pharaoh? Joseph not only interpreted the dreams but gave Pharaoh a practical application and strategy to prepare for the fulfillment of these dreams.[201] After hearing Joseph's interpretation and application, Pharaoh made Joseph second in command of Egypt to implement the plan.[202] It truly took a dreamer to restore a dreamer.

EVEN APOSTLES CAN MISS RESTORATION

The apostle Paul was quite the man of God, but no person has ever been perfect, other than the one man and Messiah, Jesus. The theology is in the literature, not just the words. Paul and Barnabas were sent out on their first missionary journey, and they brought John (a.k.a. "John Mark" or "Mark") with them.[203] This man was remarkable because he was content with doing things behind the scenes as Paul and Barnabas proclaimed the kingdom of God.[204] However, when the going became tough, John Mark got going and literally abandoned them to go back to Jerusalem.[205]

Before anyone is quick to judge, the terrain and hardships in the modern nation of Turkey, where this took place, are enough to make any traveler abandon the trip and pursue the comforts of home, especially on foot. From the tropical, mosquito-infested coast, one quickly climbs up an elevation of over ten thousand feet—and that is not even hitting the peaks! Then if we throw in robbers, temperature fluctuations, and moisture in the form of humidity, rain, and snow, most would not continue on foot. We do not have other facts on which to base John Mark's decision, but this is what he did: he abandoned his relative and ministry partners to their own devices.

Consider once again that Paul wrote, "If a man is caught in any trespass, you who are spiritual, restore such a one in a spirit of gentleness."[206] As an apostle, anyone would think that Paul would practice what he preached and follow his own teaching. It seems he was not that spiritual and even held a grudge.

Barnabas, whose name means "son of encouragement," thought that he and Paul should give John Mark a second chance and restore him to this ministry as well as their fellowship.[207] Paul would not even entertain such a concept. On the contrary, Paul became so vehemently opposed that he and Barnabas had to part ways![208] Consider this: Barnabas built Paul up and mentored him to become an apostle.[209] Barnabas was the very one to search out Saul (who became known as Paul), stand up for him, encourage him in his own faith, and get him plugged back into the body of Christ in Antioch. Yet Paul was so opposed to John Mark being restored that they parted ways—and there is not a reference of Barnabas and Paul seeing each other again.

Now as we jump back to our present age, should we be surprised when a person, a church, or a movement does not want to facilitate the restoration of a Christian brother or sister? This is the ultimate paradox. The people who should not oppose this person's restoration are the very ones who do. Instead of assisting in the restoration, they actually hinder it.

Consider Rev. Jim Bakker once again. His own movement did not facilitate his restoration to ministry. Billy Graham and his family assisted him. Rick Joyner and MorningStar Ministries brought Rev. Bakker back to preach and teach at the former Heritage, USA, campus, now Heritage International Ministries (HIM). So they literally restored this man of God; it was not his board members or his endorsing agent but influencers who were outside of his sphere of influence.

From my own experience, we must call out the paradox, the very bias any one of us has in our own soul, and realize we are not God. Perhaps we do not want to see the person restored because we just see the past failure. Every minister that I know who was removed from ministry had to leave their original endorser, church, family, town, or all of these combined, depending on the severity of the response and not necessarily the offense.

So how do we remedy this? The difficulty in providing a solution also deals with the paradox. So many aspects of a person are subjective rather than objective. We cannot merely observe healing or maturity. There is no specific time line for any particular person to be restored. We can observe fruit or actions in a person's life, but we cannot measure transformation.

Only the Holy Spirit can do this. He is the one who convicts us of sin, righteousness, and judgment.[210]

DOES ONE PROCESS WORK FOR ALL?

From the biblical as well as contemporary examples, there are several key factors in restoration. Gifts and talents continue to flow. Our gifts and our calling from God does not change.[211] The purpose of the individual does not diminish. The way in which each person is restored differs in the process. Gifts are instantaneous, but the fruit of the Spirit has to be cultivated.[212] A harvest comes through diligent application of the proper techniques. If character has been compromised or crippled, then the proper character development depends on how quickly each person is to respond to a restoration process.

Now some actions can be taken on our behalf to partner with God to pave the way for a solution. A biblical process has to be acknowledged as well as established. I am not aware of any movement that actually has a restoration framework in place. Therefore, I shall propose a framework based on the biblical examples and principles that are highlighted later.

IS THERE A TIMELINE ON RESTORATION?

Following a process, there must be some kind of probation period. The only hard part about this is we do not have a specific time line for any one person. Some people embrace a process of restoration and submit willingly and wholeheartedly. For my own father, he was in rehabilitation treatment for alcoholism over six months. Now he has not had a drink in forty-two years, praise God! As a chaplain, I have seen some people go in for six weeks of rehab and remain sober. Others have gone into treatment over longer periods of time, on more than one occasion, and still do not stick to the treatment plan and discipline that are required to walk in restoration. So in dealing with just one issue in different people, the time line is different.

Rev. Bakker has been an amazing voice in our time, and his show has had more relevancies in the last ten years than ever before. Due to his prison time, he had to work on his own issues, whether mandated by man or orchestrated by God. In looking at Rev. Bakker's life, the time line must have been right because he has been restored completely and continues to function in health and in communion with God and the body of Christ. Joseph was also placed in a prison. Whether he needed to be there or not, his character clearly transformed to the point that he was equipped to lead the Egyptian Empire through a severe famine and save the surrounding civilizations, including his own family.

The bottom line is <u>restoration is a goal, not a time line</u>. In order to meet the goal of restoration, there must be more than one person, more than the individual needing the restoration, involved in the process. The right people must be involved. We are told that there is "safety in a multitude of counselors."[213] Furthermore, if all of these "counselors" are filled with the Holy Spirit and submitted to the one who knows our heart, character, and intent, then the time line could have an adjustment.

Paraclete People

Following the process and principles, a network must be established around the people. Due to the paradox we've identified, this network may be outside of their normal network, perhaps a different denomination or oversight committee. In spending the last five years studying restoration and the kind of people identified in restoring others, I have labeled the individuals in this network as "Paraclete People," since they are walking with the Holy Spirit and walking with the client. The Holy Spirit is also called the Paraclete, the Greek term for "one who comes alongside, assists, disciples, or advocates for another."[214]

I speak from experience. I thought my pathway to ministry was shut after my public rebuke. However, my wife believed in me. Of all people, she did not allow me to stay wounded, and she continually reinforced the potential I had in God's hands and in His kingdom. She was a Paraclete Person to me in that season.

Three other people proved to be crucial in my restoration outside of the local church that I attended. First, I had a prophet named Janice Seney who spoke into my life and did not allow me to stay offended or rejected.

Second, I had a pastor in my life who taught me to follow Proverbs 4 and guard my heart above all things.[215] He also confirmed my calling and told me to pursue my current denomination, which ordained me. The third person was present in the form of a married couple who ministered to me as friends and peers. The husband stated, "The grace you give now will be the grace you receive later. You are also called as a leader and you are going to make mistakes." The love, support, and counsel from every person proved valid in my life.

THE HEARTBEAT OF GOD

Given the amount of narrative, revelation, and prophecy concerning restoration, there is no doubt that this is the heartbeat of God. Peter declared:

> But the things which God announced beforehand by the mouth of all the prophets, that His Christ should suffer, He has thus fulfilled. Repent therefore and return, that your sins may be wiped away, in order that times of refreshing may come from the presence of the Lord; and that He may send Jesus, the Christ appointed for you, whom heaven must receive until the period of restoration of all things about which God spoke by the mouth of His holy prophets from ancient time.[216]

apokatastasis

When it comes to Scripture, the theology is in the literature, along with the context and the historical and cultural backgrounds. In this passage, the repetition of the *mouth of the prophets* indicates that everything sandwiched between them is important. The phrase *times of refreshing* comes from the Greek words for "opportune times"[217] and "recovery of breath."[218] Notice that these opportune times are plural. The idea of "recovery of breath" is where we historically use the word *revival*, but this word is intentional, with this sole use in the entire New Testament. "Recovery of breath" can refer to someone recovering after a long run or journey, or it can relate to recovery of a lost life, as in resuscitation.

The Greek word used in "period of restoration of all things" is *chronos*, as in a chronological period of time.[219] So as we are aiming for a period of restoration, recovery opportunities will present themselves. However, people are the main focus when it comes to recovery.

Whether it is Rev. Jim Bakker or John Mark or the member in our community who has been caught in a trespass, the opportunities to recover a brother or sister will appear. Even the apostle Paul proved that it takes the Holy Spirit to overcome our own perspective or judgments. So if some people are not keen on the idea of recovering a brother or sister, but you are the "spiritual" one, then do what you can to recover such a person and restore them within the body of Christ and within the community. If we are to be known by our love, it will show in our ability to restore people to their place of purpose.

Points to Ponder

1. From your perspective, who have you seen restored, and how did this occur?
2. Have you ever felt like things will turn around on a certain time line, but they did not?
3. Have you ever heard someone else's dream and thought it might imply to you?
4. How do you think you can remedy the paradox in your sphere of influence, where members of the body of Christ seem to not want to facilitate restoration?
5. Are you a Paraclete Person, willing to assist in the restoration of people?

7

RESTORATION IN A NEW GENERATION

Deferred hope makes the heart sick, but a longing fulfilled is a tree of life.[220]

So what do we do if a paradox may actually have a possible truth? I wrote earlier concerning the definition of a paradox and focused on the second definition. Now let us consider the first definition of a *paradox*: "a statement or proposition that seems self-contradictory or absurd but in reality expresses a possible truth."[221] People are limited by time, but God is not. God has eternity as a perspective and knows the end from the beginning. Perhaps somebody else must complete the restoration and God has a purpose for it in the next generation? This may be a paradox for us but not for God. God considers all of the generations. Perhaps this is why God revealed Himself as the "God of Abraham, the God of Isaac, and the God of Jacob."[222]

God's heart for restoration never stops beating. Even if we do not perceive it or understand how this will work out, His system and ways of accounting go beyond time. God is not limited by time. To the Lord, a thousand years is like a day.[223] On the opposite end of time, God's grace can accomplish something in one day that transforms the entire world. Jesus dying on the cross is an example of this phenomenon. Additionally, righteousness and justice are a part of God's throne.[224] God is always right, and His justice is always pure. His judgments are true.[225] With this perspective, we can confidently pray for His judgments to come. If God said it will happen, then it will come to pass, even if it does not fall within our timetable.

Sometimes the paradox twists in the fabric of time in ways beyond our comprehension. God can judge when the opportune time aligns with the restoration that fulfills a number of things converging at one time. People are limited in their understanding due to their temporal existence and limited information. Job thought he could question God in His ways, but God had a way of making Job realize that all of His accounting system is audited without a single mistake. In the end, Job not only had everything restored, but saw God double his restoration and lived to see his descendants to the fourth generation.[226] God can do the same thing in our lives.

ISRAELITES IN AND OUT OF EGYPT

God spoke to Abraham about his descendants. Even though God promised Abraham the land of Israel, he was not going to be the one to fully possess the promise. His descendants would obtain the promise but only after a lengthy time of slavery. The Lord told him his offspring would be enslaved for four hundred years![227] This would not exactly fit the American dream. Most people would be inclined to argue with God about justice if it came to this kind of plan. Yet, in God's eyes, this was not even half a day. Since God is also righteous, He had a reason to redeem the land because of the sin and iniquity within it. Of course, four hundred years of descendants did not understand this or get to partake of it. This did not seem fair to them. But God heard their cry and rose up a deliverer. Generations had cycled through their lives, but the restoration plan received fulfillment on God's timetable.

Why did the Israelites remain in Egypt after the famine? Joseph interpreted Pharaoh's dreams correctly in predicting seven years of abundance followed by seven years of famine.[228] This set Joseph apart from everyone else. No one else but Joseph could interpret the dreams.[229] After his interpretations, Joseph was restored to a place of prominence as second in command of Egypt.[230] Given Joseph's position, he still retained power after the famine.

Following Jacob's death, Joseph's brothers begged for their lives because of Joseph having preeminence.[231] Joseph reassured his brothers and went with them into the land of Canaan to bury their father. So why did they not leave Egypt with their families at this time? The Bible does not give a reason. Perhaps human nature kicked in. People stay where they are so long as they are comfortable.

One thing must be certain: the Jewish people did not stay in Egypt just to fulfill the prophecy given to Abraham about his descendants being enslaved for four hundred years. Thanks to Joseph, the Israelites must have had all they wanted in place to enjoy life enough to settle in Goshen. The Israelites remained in Egypt long enough so that the new king did not learn what Joseph did.[232] The Egyptians turned favor into enslavement, and the comfortable existence disappeared. The Israelites began to cry out to God, and He heard them.[233] In this generation, things were about to change.

When Moses came on the scene, He was not what the Israelites were expecting. The first time he tried to deliver the Israelites, his own people thought he might kill them like he had killed an Egyptian.[234] This caused a forty-year delay in anything happening. After God appeared to Moses and instructed him to go back to Egypt, freedom would not come without a fight. After the ten plagues released by God through Moses had decimated the Egyptians and their lands, the Egyptians released them.

The Israelites received favor with the Egyptians and obtained payment for their four hundred years of labor.[235] Therefore, this generation under the oversight of Moses received all the resources at once. If the Jewish people had believed the good report of the two spies, Joshua and Caleb, they would have even received the land promised to Abraham.

God could get the Israelites out of Egypt, but He could not get the people to let go of Egypt in their heart. Due to their grumbling and unbelief, the people of God had to wait another generation before they could go in and possess the land.[236] That younger generation did go into the land, led by two men, Joshua and Caleb, from the previous generation.

Joshua and Caleb received the fulfillment of Abraham's promise, but they did have to fight for it. In Caleb's case, the land promised to him by Moses had giants living in it, but he still went to face them.[237] God enabled Caleb to overcome giants at the age of eighty-five; God sustained him, and he was able to go to war like he had done in his youth.[238] Since God shows no partiality, He will do the same thing for us if we choose to contend for the restoration due within our generation. He will protect us and keep us in supernatural ways, going beyond human reasoning. Restoration is a huge deal to God and in the generations when the opportune time has come.

ISRAELITES OUT OF BABYLON

God desires to restore people, even when it is their sin getting them into dire straits. This goes back to Adam, when he disobeyed God and ate of the Tree of the Knowledge of Good and Evil.[239] It was the only tree from which he was forbidden to eat the fruit. After this disobedience, God sacrificed animals to cover the nakedness of the humans and to indicate the shedding of blood needed to atone for sin.[240] God was already making a way for restoration. Adam and Eve were expelled from the Garden of Eden to ensure they did not eat from the Tree of Life and stay separated from God forever.[241] Before Jesus went to the cross, humanity had a propensity to sin. In Christ, people have a propensity to righteousness by becoming a new creation.[242] Christians also receive the Holy Spirit convicting them of righteousness, judgment, and sin.[243]

God had sent numerous prophets to the nation of Israel, but they continued to rebel against God and eventually brought about their own expulsion on a national level. Samaria and the northern kingdom of Israel fell to the Assyrian Empire more than a hundred years prior to Jerusalem and the kingdom of Judah. Jeremiah the prophet declared that Jerusalem and the southern kingdom of Judah would be captured. In 586 BC, the Babylonian Kingdom under Nebuchadnezzar captured Jerusalem and left some people behind but took the temple items, the treasures, and the best people of the land.[244]

Jeremiah also gave a time line for the Babylonian captivity. Due to not fulfilling the Sabbaths ascribed by the law, God said the land would receive seventy years of rest.[245] Once again, seven represents completeness—and this at tenfold. God is the Great Accountant. He has a way of accounting for all of our sins. His grace also accounted for the sin of the entire world by having them paid for on a cross. Another generation would be able to experience God's restoration.

Just one person can make a difference when it comes to God's heartbeat for restoration. Jeremiah prophesied Israel's restoration to the land, not just its captivity.[246] Since these were recorded, anyone with an education and access could read it. Daniel, being educated in all literature, may very well have read this prophecy.[247] For a number of reasons, Daniel set out to seek God. Daniel received a message about Israel's restoration from Gabriel after praying and confessing the sin of his people.[248] God was confirming that His plan for restoration had not changed.

More than one hundred years before Cyrus was even born, Isaiah prophesied Cyrus's existence as well as his purpose. God was going to use Cyrus, a person outside of the covenant people of God, to enable the restoration of Israel through his position of leadership.[249] Perhaps Daniel had read this as well. Daniel realized a convergence within his generation was unfolding. His prayers and repentance were just as active in the restoration process as Ezra's and Nehemiah's efforts with a hammer and chisel in Jerusalem. The restoration process in our generation takes action. We cannot simply be passive and think it will happen. We must participate with God at the level He is requiring of us. This includes being purposed in the right place at the right time.

A WOMAN AT THE WELL

God had a much greater agenda in mind for restoring the people to the land following seventy years of exile. God's idea of restoration narrows down to working out the right conditions for just one woman at a well centuries later. He began setting things up when the patriarchs wandered through the land of Canaan in tents. God had lined things up over forty generations earlier; only He could do something like this.

Some details do not get recorded the way we would like. Genesis does not record a well being dug, but Jacob lived near Shechem "and bought a plot of land."[250] So Jacob already obtained a piece of the promise in his generation. In Jacob's era, water had to be found if a family wanted to settle on a plot of land. The reference to Jacob's well in John 4 indicated something occurred near the ancient city of Shechem.[251] Whether this was passed down through an oral tradition or revelation to John, he referred to this specific well as Jacob's well. Jacob did not know how significant the location was going to be for a well, but God did.

Have you ever wondered why the genealogy of Jesus gets listed at the beginning of Matthew? In total, three groupings of fourteen generations get named in the natural genealogy of Jesus.[252] The number has significance. As a factor of seven, fourteen also indicates completeness. But fourteen also signifies "salvation and rescue in addition to a double of God's power and completion."[253] So from the time of Jacob, forty generations have passed, which is the number for testing. God was not being tested, but perhaps the plan for total restoration was.

John was unique in his gospel, not only because it was written much later than the other gospels, but because he recorded aspects of Jesus's life and ministry the others did not even reference. The Samaritan woman at the well happens to be one of those stories.[254] One might ask, why her? Due to the interracial mix with the Assyrian people who occupied this land, the Samaritans were considered inferior to the "pure" Jewish people who dwelt in Jerusalem and the southern region outside of Samaria. Racism is not a new concept by any means. Yet John picked this story to show "the restoration of all things," including a woman who did not fit the narrative of what people thought God would choose to redeem.[255]

This Samaritan woman happened to live within the same time line as Jesus—forty generations after Jacob dug the well near Shechem. So how many details needed to line up in order for Jesus, the Son of Man, to interact with this Samaritan woman at this well? I am not a statistician, but my guess would be the statistics would reveal astronomical odds that this encounter would even happen. But God ensured that it did. We were told that "Jesus only did what He saw the Father doing."[256] So God had this woman on His heart when Jacob dug a well. If God would do this for the Samaritan woman, what is He willing to do for you and me?

THE NATION OF ISRAEL

After six years of genocide and tragedy, an environment was synergized through politics, compassion, and empathy. A surviving generation witnessed the establishment of Israel as a nation on May 14, 1948. Not surprisingly, President Harry S. Truman was the first leader of a nation to acknowledge the Jewish state of Israel. Given the vast population of Jewish people throughout its states and territories, along with its Judeo-Christian heritage, the most powerful nation on the world scene gave its blessing and approval to the nation. After nearly two thousand years, the nation of Israel officially existed again. This restoration culminated the hopes and prayers of the generations spanning this entire era.

In this current generation, what is God indicating? The United States was the first nation to acknowledge Israel as a free state on May 14, 1948. The United States was the first nation to recognize Jerusalem as the legitimate capital of Israel, and in 2018, it dedicated its new American embassy on the seventieth anniversary of Israel as a nation on May 14. The number seven represents completeness, but here it represents completeness in a way that matches the seventy years spanning between Israel's Babylonian captivity and the people's restoration to their homeland. Every matter—which is the Greek word *rhema*—is established by the testimony of two or three witnesses.[257] Only God could get this to line up decades apart. As the God who is eternal and transcendent, He cares deeply for the restoration of every person, tribe, ethnic group, and nation through all generations.

Due to the recent events and the biblical prophecies, Israel has been a great example to illustrate what God is willing to do in one nation through the generations. The same principle applies for every person, group, and nation on this planet. God's heart for restoration is for us. He desires to see all things restored the way they are meant to be, according to His desires, plans, and purposes. Even after rampant sin and disobedience, God's mercy and compassion get extended through the generations.[258] Israel was not meant to be the exception but the pattern to demonstrate God's heart to work through the lineage of one family through the generations. The same principle applies to places as well.

JERICHO

When the Israelites entered the Promised Land, the first city they conquered was Jericho. People were forbidden to take anything out of the city because this was the "first fruits" of their possession, which are to be offered to the LORD.[259] This is why Achan's sin, taking things meant for the LORD's treasury, was so egregious to the LORD. On top of this, Joshua cursed anyone who restored the city with the death of their firstborn as well as their youngest son.[260] So why would someone be moved to restore such a city?

The question does not get answered, at least not in the time frame of the Hebrew Scriptures. First Kings 16 tells us that Hiel of Bethel restored Jericho, but the author did not give a valid reason he did this at the cost of his two sons.[261] Hiel's name means "living of God," signifying his relationship with the one true God.[262] Bethel means "house of God," which was defined within Jacob's encounter with the LORD and viewing the ladder going into heaven with angels ascending and descending.[263] For a man to leave the "house of God" while "living [for] God," some divine purpose must have motivated Hiel, even with such a cost to his family.

Hiel did not have an idea of who would walk through the city or who would be blessed, but God did. In addition to the city's restoration, the waters of Jericho received restoration. Elisha the prophet came to Jericho in 2 Kings 2 and was confronted by the men of the city, who told him the water was bad and that the ground was barren because of it.[264] Elisha took a new bowl with salt in it and cast it into the water source, declaring, "Thus says the LORD: 'I have healed this water; from it there shall be no more death or barrenness.'"[265] Now why would God move through a prophet to heal the water and land of this city?

Elisha saw a lot of things and performed several miracles, but he probably did not realize the Christ would wander through the streets of Jericho. Neither did Hiel, but God knew the significance of the city. Jesus could walk down to Jericho because the city was a part of the Jewish district. He did just that, as we read in Mark 10. On His way into the city, a blind man named Bartimaeus heard the commotion and asked what was happening. When Bartimaeus heard Jesus was passing by, he cried out for Jesus to heal him. Due to a city restoration generations before he was born, Bartimaeus received his sight.[266] Because Jericho had been restored, Zacchaeus, too, had an encounter with Jesus on the street. Zacchaeus not only encountered Jesus but had the Messiah invite Himself to dine at Zacchaeus's house.[267] All of this was made possible by the restoration of Jericho in another generation completely oblivious to the significance of this moment in time.

GOD OF THE GENERATIONS

Whether it was the Jewish people or other cities and nations, God's plan for restoration and redemption gets orchestrated perfectly. God's heart for the generations comes through the restoration. When God called for a deliverer to set the Israelites free from bondage through Moses, He revealed Himself as "the God of your father—the God of Abraham, the God of Isaac, and the God of Jacob."[268] God revealed Himself as the Generational God.

What does God want to do in our family lineage? "God shows no partiality."[269] If He will do something for one family, then He will certainly do it for another. Perhaps one of us has gone through a loss that goes beyond our capability to recover in our lifetime. In the midst of the 2020 coronavirus condition, followed by the riots, some people lost everything. But what if God has orchestrated a restoration project within our family line that began two or three generations ago, and it is going to catch up to us in our lifetime? The Israelites who did leave Egypt had the payment in full for all of their generations working as slaves. God accounted for every day. Our breakthrough in our lives could be the result of God working a restoration project going back in decades or even centuries when the family has no record.

Ask God to reveal what is being restored in your generation. Whether this is for your family, your church, your city, or your nation, see what comes to light and how you can join God in the process. The best things in life are worth fighting for and waiting for. Through faith and patience, we inherit the promises.[270] In a culture filled with instant gratification, delayed gratification has lost its luster. God truly has our best interests in mind, and He will make His goodness come before us when it will produce the most fruitfulness. None of us are forgotten, so embrace the process and engage with Him where He wants to restore.

POINTS TO PONDER

1. Why did the Israelites remain in Egypt after the famine?
2. What does God want to do in our family lineage?
3. What is God restoring in your generation?
4. Have you ever wondered why the genealogy of Jesus gets listed at the beginning of Matthew?
5. In this generation, what is God indicating?
6. If God would do this for the Samaritan woman, what is He willing to do for you and me?
7. What if God began a restoration project within our family line that began two or three generations ago, and it is going to catch up to us in our lifetime?

This chapter is essentially IHE

8

RESTORATION OF A VISION

Write the vision and make it plain on tablets, that he may run who reads it.[271]

For those of us possessing eyesight, how would our lives be different if we could not see anymore? For those of us old enough to drive, we would certainly lose our social mobility. If the loss were instantaneous, we would have to adapt to reading another language called Braille or rely on others to always read for us. We would have to arrange all of our clothes in a certain order along with our money, toiletries, and anything else. After working in a level 1 trauma center in the Denver area, I have witnessed firsthand how the loss of sight can be upsetting, at a minimum. Natural vision provides a unique perspective to the world around us. For those of us who have vision without any hindrance, we can appreciate the sunrise and the sunset and everything between the two.

So what happens to us if we have no vision or imagination to perceive a better future? What if a businessman cannot conceive a final product before it is even designed? How would an author finish a book if the concept for a captive audience could not be imagined? People without natural vision but who possess spiritual vision are much better off than those who have perfect eyesight but have no foresight. Without a prophetic revelation, we will perish due to the lack of restraint leading to wasted resources along with a wasted life.[272] In order for restoration to be possible, we must obtain a revelation from God of what the final result will be, whether this is a person, a city, or a nation.

The ability to exercise foresight can pay huge dividends in the business world. When we understand Pharaoh's wisdom of installing Joseph as the person to oversee the administration of his kingdom to survive the famine following the years of abundance, we perceive that Joseph exercised foresight by indicating the kind of restraint an entire kingdom would need to practice. When it comes to restoration, this kind of foresight must view the results for the long haul. In building a city like Constantinople, the builders had to think generationally because they would not see the final product themselves. The building program in that city lasted for five or more generations. Furthermore, they wanted it to stand for at least a thousand years. Their theology and vision was reflected in the architecture. Both foresight and prophetic revelation had to be exercised to build the Hagia Sophia, the Christian basilica that was built nearly 1,500 years ago and still stands today.

OBTAINING A VISION

For many of us, out of everything we'll cover in this book, the most difficult aspect can be obtaining a vision. Since we need the inspiration of God, we are on His timetable. We do not know if we will get it all at once or if He will deliver the plan in pieces. So, we not only have to be in a receiving mode, we have to be fluid in watching for how the vision comes, because flexible is still too rigid. Upon obtaining a vision, we also want clarity, with everything clearly defined up front. But sometimes, the clarity comes as we embrace the revelation God has entrusted to us.

God's heart for restoration resides within a vision. The biggest question for any of us would be, "How close to the original design do you want this?" When the temple was being restored, the sound of the rejoicing could not be distinguished from the weeping because those who remembered the former glory grieved the design being less than the original.[273] This does not diminish the restoration in any way. When I was working on my 1965 Barracuda, I wanted to keep it to the original design and original parts. But a coworker won awards on his 1936 Ford as a *restomod*—restored plus modifications—since he added more current technology with a V8 engine. God wants us to partner with Him in how the finished product will appear in the process and turn out in the end.

RECORDING A VISION

Once we are in a receiving mode, we must also have a recording mode. The quote at the beginning of the chapter from Habakkuk 2 was not just meant to be a good social media post. This was God's instruction to the prophet Habakkuk, who was also receiving a vision from God about restoration. Writing the vision down was not just for Habakkuk to be able to run with it. The recording was meant for anyone who read the vision and received the charge to continue in the restoration until it was complete. Verse 3 of Habakkuk 2 states, "For the vision is yet for an appointed time; but at the end it will speak, and it will not lie. Though it tarries, wait for it; because it will surely come, it will not delay."[274] Recorded visions get fulfilled.

In our era, educational studies and professional habits have proven the Bible to be true. When people write down what they imagine for the future, it becomes a goal. If we "envision our future, then we bring it toward us."[275] We have been gifted with the power of an imagination for a reason. When we can articulate this future into a goal, we are drawing that future to become our present. We must also "begin with the end in mind" when we create our goal.[276] If we cannot perceive the final project, then we will not complete the goal, let alone start it. Many a sculptor or wood carver can view the final product in mind before they make the first cut.

In the military, we learn to set goals, whether this is going to be short-term, like for one enlistment, or a plan to continue through an entire career. We are taught goals must be SMART.[277] We are better off being smart, too, but this acronym makes it easy to remember. If you recall, this stands for specific, measurable, attainable, realistic, and time-specific.[278] All of these facets give us guidelines for how we will achieve the goal—or, in our case, the restoration.

Thanks to all of our modern technology, we can record and design numerous things with virtual technology, making the process interactive. With God, His goal involves engagement on every level. One of my best friends is a highly skilled architect who has a virtual viewing area. A client can wear virtual reality (VR) goggles and get a "walkthrough" of a building before the cornerstone is even laid. We have the capacity to record our visions, our dreams, and our plans in amazing detail. When this comes to people, we can create the goal of helping them achieve their divine potential and make it detailed with regard to the person's mental, emotional, social, spiritual, financial, and positional well-being.

RECOVERING A VISION

If I wanted to account for the number of times a vision, plan, or goal was recorded and then completely destroyed, the resulting book would be like the *Penguin History of the World*, which has well over a thousand pages. In my own life, I have had to reset a goal hundreds of times. Technology has made things easier to record and keep a record, but things can still be completely lost. For those of us who are Christian, the good news is we can consult God, who has a heart for restoration. He functions with the highest creativity and "created us in His likeness and image."[279] So we can be like Him and create what was conceived in our heart. The good news for us is that it is easier to edit our work than it is to create. If we have already taken the time to create something, the memory has an amazing capacity to reproduce the same pattern.

Even God had to recover a vision for creation, which is why Jesus went to the cross. Before this, Moses had to recreate the stone tablets for the Ten Commandments because he threw them down when he witnessed the Israelite camp engulfed in sin and idolatry.[280] Whether our own mistakes or the actions of others have caused an original vision to be lost, God has a way of working through every circumstance, enabling us to accomplish His will.

If we get concerned about recovering the vision in a timely manner, God has His hands in that as well. Whether God is in the delay or will use the delay, He is never late in His plan. We get the joy of seeing how the vision unfolds. "The vision is yet for an appointed time; but at the end it will speak and it will not lie. Though it tarries, wait for it; because it will surely come, it will not delay."[281] We just need to press into God, and He will surely give us the ability to perceive the vision. We will have the vision come to pass at the appointed time.

COUNTING THE COST

As much as we would like to get things back to the way they were, the restoration is not as quick as the loss. When the Waldo Canyon Fire swept through Colorado Springs in 2012, many families wanted to begin rebuilding even as the embers were still burning. The original designs were still available. However, due to mass destruction, the price of lumber, copper, and brick went up sharply because of the demand on the supply. So many things can change overnight that we do not anticipate.

When Jesus addressed a crowd about discipleship, He actually discussed planning to see whether the listeners had the capability to follow through to completion. Jesus stated, "For which of you intending to build a tower, does not sit down first and count the cost, whether he has enough to finish it."[282] This does not just refer to resources but to time and discipline as well.

We must know both our capabilities and our limitations. If we are not good at a task like concrete work for pouring a house foundation, we must know how much it will cost to hire the right masons and determine the right amount of cement. Due to limits with supplies, reconstruction can also be delayed. This is where our discipline must be set. If we get insurance money for a house that burned down, but we spend it on a new truck, how can we afford to rebuild the house?

On July 29, 2016, we had baseball- to softball-sized hail hit Cheyenne, Wyoming. Practically every roof in the city had to be replaced. Due to the demand, our roof repair could not be scheduled until June of the following year. Instead of spending the insurance money, we paid the $6,000 deposit to the roofing company to ensure it would get accomplished and guarantee the money did not go to something else. Sometimes, we must make an investment up front to make a vision become a reality.

Now how do we count the cost when it comes to restoring a person? How much time will it take for a person like Rev. Bakker? How many disciplines will be involved? Where will the person be housed? How will we decide when this person is ready to be released? Who will provide a probationary placement in order to assess the restoration? In Rev. Bakker's case, we know it came slowly but steadily. He was not instantly back on television, but he is there now. Every person is absolutely worth the time and resources, but the cost must be considered.

IMPLEMENTING A VISION

None of us ever plan to fail. But if we fail to plan, then we know what the result will be. If we take a vision or plan and run with it, we must be able to break it down into steps. This is why we must know our abilities and our limits. If we are not good at breaking something down into actionable steps, we may need to rely on another person's skills. I have good news for us all.

God designed us to be interdependent, rather than dependent or independent. Here is where it pays off to be a part of a community. We cannot do all things on our own. We all start out as a baby. Other parts of the body can supply what a particular part needs.[283] Some of us are visionaries and are great at seeing concepts, both short-term and long-term. Then others in our community are great at the details and breaking things down into the smallest tasks. Whether a person, a business, a city, or a nation requires restoration, we are meant to work as a team in order to implement a vision. We are created for interdependence by design.

SOARING WITH VISION

The environment has a way of forming us as well as informing us. Where I was raised, we had two seasons: winter and construction. When we drove through a road construction area, we wondered how they kept going when the old road was torn out and there was nothing but mud and gravel in the ditch to get by all the workers and equipment. And with that part of the country being both Tornado Alley and Hail Alley, we average seven to nine days of hail every year. Yet, every year, the civil engineers' plans have been accomplished by the construction foremen and their crews. Due to some adverse circumstances, they may experience some delays, but they still finish before winter sets in again.

We have different people who have different strengths in demonstrating resiliency. In the midst of all of our thunderstorms in Hail Alley, we have the opportunity to watch golden eagles and bald eagles soar on the updrafts of the storms. These beautiful birds certainly know what the view is like from fifteen thousand feet.

During storms of life, certain people actually excel in crisis. Former president Bush was one of these individuals after the terrorist tacks of 9/11. Habakkuk stated God's instruction to "record the vision so he may run who reads it."[284] Let me emphasize the word *run* here. Whether this is on a personal scale or a national scale, someone can pick up the vision and run with it with a grand perspective. As author John P. Kotter states, "Vision is one of the four main qualities of a leader in what must be imparted as well as instilled."[285] When it comes to dealing with vision, the person who can impart or instill the vision into the people around them will be the one to rise up among us.

FROM VISION TO REALITY

Going from a concept to construction—or reconstruction, in many cases—involves a process. When Paul wrote, "we are being transformed from glory to glory," the longest word in concept form referring to time and process is *to*.[286] For the Israelites coming out of Egypt, this was forty years. For the Israelites coming back out of Babylonian captivity, we have another seventy years. For Christians who prayed for deliverance living under the Soviet regime, it was seventy-five years, from 1917 to 1992, before the transformation came. Whether the *to* is personal or corporate, local or national, the vision must be gained to endure and oversee the restoration to completion.

If a dream or vision was lost due to a disaster, either natural or human-manufactured, we must seek God for resurrection. It does not matter if it was our childhood dream and we are now approaching retirement age. God has proven repeatedly through history that He can restore dreams and renew our hope. It is all right to tell our hearts to dream again.

A famous architect, Tadao Ando, gives us a clue of what a process can look like from start to finish.[287] Before Mr. Ando begins to design a building, he will spend a year in that area to understand how it will stand out or blend in with the surrounding architecture through every season. Mr. Ando has a "unique way of combining concrete, space, and light."[288] The concept of light comes through in more ways than one.

When we receive illumination, clarity comes, and we can clearly see the path lying ahead. This is why the "path of life gets brighter and brighter until noon."[289] Mr. Ando started out as a boxer, but his interest and passion took him on a completely different path. As Christians, we may not always see the path clearly, but this is how the body of Christ was designed: one part of the body may supply what another part is lacking. So we have a way of not only gaining our vision but recovering our vision. Then we can count what the cost will be and start planning according to the vision.

Now imagine the process for restoring a person who needs spirit, soul, and body restored to functioning in a healthy way. Every person is unique, so a cookie-cutter formula will not work when it comes to the particular process and timing they will undergo. We will need to grasp a vision for the person if they have been tossed out of every community or place of influence. God's desire is to use every person because He is the best steward of all. He wants every one of us to fulfill our purpose and reach our full potential. We must hold on to this as a starting point for every vision in order to run with it. God is the best architect of all and has a design in mind. So let us go for the ultimate high calling for every person, city, and nation.

POINTS TO PONDER

1. So, what happens to us if we have no vision or imagination to perceive a better future?
2. What is the opportunity cost if we spend insurance money or an inheritance on our own desires without consulting God?
3. How would we count the cost when it comes to restoring a person?
4. Do you perceive God removing a delay, being in a delay, or using a delay in your situation?

9

RESTORATION OF A CITY

> Those from among you shall build the old waste places;
> you shall raise up the foundations of many generations;
> and you shall be called the repairer of the breach, the
> restorer of streets to dwell in.[290]

Cities must be as important to God as they are to humanity. Cities are truly unique, like snowflakes. They can be a similar size or zoned in a similar way, but every one of them has something unique. Each city seems to emit a certain character or personality because they were established to make people who dwell there feel like they are a part of something bigger than just themselves or their particular family. Cities have a way of attracting people to them without saying a word. Interestingly, cities are not living organisms, yet they receive references like *lively, the city that never sleeps,* or *dead.* Nobody wants to live in a "dying" or "dead" city. This is why restoration becomes paramount for people who have a heart to see their respective cities thrive again.

From historical records to biblical passages, cities have risen up as an important aspect of civilization. Two of the first terms used in reference to the first city reveal some significant details.[291] Remember, the law of first mention establishes the precedent for the term where it appears in any other passage. The first term for *city* means "awake," in the sense of watching over it like a guard.[292] As I mentioned before, in order to be "lively," one must be awake and active. When we think about it, enough people had to be present where someone could remain awake while the others rested. The second word used for a city was *Enoch*, which means "dedicated."[293] Every city is dedicated to someone or something; hence the name bears significance for every other city. So when a city gets devastated, it is not just about the city being restored solely for occupation but rather for the aspect it represents.

In this chapter, we will focus on four cities for personal and symbolic reasons. A number of other cities could be used, including the particular city each of us comes from, where our home resides, or where we have seen devastation on an astronomical scale. But before we examine each of these towns, we'll explore the biblical concepts leading to the major restoration to establish a precedent in restoring our cities.

FAITH AND FORTRESS

If we are still skeptical about the importance of cities and God's desire to see them restored, consider the Word of God. Two books in the Bible focus on the restoration of Jerusalem. The book of Ezra focuses on the rebuilding of the temple, while Nehemiah chronicles the restoration of the city walls, gates, and infrastructure. As believers, we can see the significance of each. We are part of an unshakeable kingdom, but things on this earth, including cities, can undergo destruction beyond a shaking. As a testimony of God's faithfulness, a rebuilding of the city and restoration of its significance must be implemented.

When it came to faith in the ancient Near East, a god was considered to be tied to the land. With the Israelites, this remained true, and it still stands today. The temple in Jerusalem was dedicated to the God of Abraham, Isaac, and Jacob, who made a covenant promising the land to them and their descendants forever.[294] The destruction of the first temple and the city crumbled not only the Jewish kingdom but also their faith. Restoration became a spiritual priority before it became a physical priority.

Daniel was mentioned previously, but his character and actions are very important in restoration. Daniel studied all literature, including the Jewish sacred texts, and came to Jeremiah's prophecy.[295] When Daniel learned God had a plan for restoration, he initiated the process through prayer, fasting, and indentificational repentance. *Identificational repentance* is identifying with the sins of your ancestors or nation and requesting that God remove the iniquity caused by their actions, even if we did not participate in it.[296] Daniel paved the way spiritually for what Ezra and Nehemiah would complete physically. These men would also experience resistance on a spiritual and natural level, but the breakthrough to restoration began with Daniel.

Before Daniel, another prophet delivered a similar pattern that led to restoration. The theology lies within the literature. In Isaiah 58, the prophet began with repentance and fasting. But then the focus turned to assisting others who needed healing and restoration.[297] In essence, the people can reap what they sow. The path becomes brighter and leads to restoration of the generations and the city.[298] But Isaiah did not stop there. If the people of God restored the Sabbath to its proper place, they would "delight in the LORD and ride on the high hills of the earth."[299] Thus faith becomes the foundation for all restoration as people of God. Unless the LORD builds the house or the fortress, every laborer's work becomes futile.[300] We want to partner with God in the work every step of the way.

JERUSALEM

Historically and spiritually, some cities have an eternal priority that cannot be erased. Jerusalem, the first of the four cities we will study, represents a foundation to three major world religions. Even though Ezra and Nehemiah covered the restoration of the temple and city within Jerusalem, these books only covered one of the restorations that happened for this city following the destruction after the siege in 586 BC. Due to its location, the city had been conquered by the Greeks, Romans, and Muslims, to name a few. The destruction after the Roman conquest in AD 70 caused the destruction of the Jewish temple, which has not been rebuilt to this date.

Considering the number of times Jerusalem has changed hands, it is incredible that the city still stands. Depending on the ethnicity, religion, or empire ruling the city, the emphasis on the city's restoration has varied. The most significant events for Jerusalem have unfolded in the last century. The Jewish people had not controlled the Holy City since their independence under the Maccabean Revolt leading up to the Hasmonean dynasty in 160 BC.[301] The time of Jewish control was short-lived due to the Roman annexation of the territory shortly after this.

The restoration of Jerusalem under Israelite control following the Roman occupation lingered for nearly two thousand years, when they took over the city along with all the territory from the Mediterranean Sea to the Jordan River in the Six-Day War.[302] The Jewish people would then fight for another fifty years politically before their historical and religious capital got official recognition. President Trump did what previous American presidents had promised for the previous twenty years when he recognized the city of Jerusalem, rather than Tel Aviv, as the Jewish capital, and the American embassy officially relocated to Jerusalem on the country's seventieth anniversary, May 14, 2018.

Just as Nehemiah and his men had to be armed in order to restore the city, the city of Jerusalem took some contending to get to its rightful restoration. Anything worth complete restoration can involve the fight of our lives. As indicated, the full restoration may not be realized in our lifetime, but it is meant to be a generational process. The process does not just stop once the restoration occurs; it continues in order to hold on to it and maintain it. None of us know how much faith and prayer went into this miracle of Jerusalem's establishment as the Israeli capital happening in our lifetime. The reward for overcoming the greatest obstacles can come by being a part of the complete fulfillment. With a restoration project on this kind of scale, we have a great reason to shout for joy. Within Judeo-Christian communities, we are commanded to pray for the peace of Jerusalem.[303] The culmination of centuries of contending for the designation of Jerusalem as the capital of Israel has come to fruition. This significant restoration carries a future hope and great expectations for millions of believers.

Lemmon, South Dakota

The second city used as an example for restoration may be unheard of for many of you. When I use the term *city*, I am not just referring to a huge metropolis. For people in the United States or Canada, this can refer to any town having a zip code. I was raised in Hettinger, North Dakota, which had a population of less than two thousand people when I lived there. Just across the border east and southward, about twenty-five miles away, the town of Lemmon, South Dakota, had a similar size but some distinct features. Their Petrified Park, the world's largest petrified wood park, still stands out in my mind today.

Like many small towns in the west, Lemmon was a dying town, with many of the stores closing and jobs disappearing. Other than the agriculture industry and a few supporting businesses, not much remained. The domino effect caused the kids who grew up in the area to go to college and find a job in a metropolitan area, not returning to an already struggling city. Lemmon was truly turning into a "lemon." But then God happened.

Lemmon may have been dying as a town, but God happened to send a young(er) evangelist named Jason Adair, who answered the call and came to a remote, unlikely place. In a town with few people attending a church, one does not go there for the money. Only true motives based on a true call from God would cause someone to go to a place like this. Thanks be to God, Jason not only went, he contended and stayed. After six months, the town was transformed spiritually.

This was not just about Pentecostals or Presbyterians or Catholics increasing their flocks. The denominational walls fell down, and the kingdom of God was the new normal in the area. New facilities had to be built, but not just so "their own people" could attend. When all these denominations came together in unity to both worship and pray, something significant happened by the power of the Holy Spirit. People were healed physically. The land was healed, too, so ranchers in the surrounding area actually made a profit and did not lose their family farms, some that had been with them for five generations.

In a natural way, God resurrected the fledgling town. Things started to happen besides church construction projects. Some businesses moved into the area, and, partly due to the draw of people, a couple of bigger hotels changed the demographics. With a surge in outdoor activities, like the best pheasant hunting in the world, the town now receives more than its fair share of visitors. If a person is spiritually sensitive, the atmosphere lingers with a peace, hope, and joy going beyond natural senses.

Following this move of God, a major film even opened in Lemmon. *The Revenant*, with Leonardo DiCaprio playing Hugh Glass, launched the 2016 motion picture year.[304] Great action movies can really set the tone for what people watch throughout the rest of the year. While it's not remarkable for a little-known town to have their Petrified Park or fishing and wildlife wonders close by, a high-budget film opening up in Lemmon—a town with less than two thousand people—this was a huge deal.[305] For those who remember events from twenty years earlier, this was actually a God deal.

HIROSHIMA

Numerous cities around the world have experienced utter devastation. But only two cities in the world have been hit with a nuclear bomb: Hiroshima and Nagasaki. The third city for our consideration is Hiroshima. Following something so destructive, with radiation fallout as a concern for years, why was restoring Hiroshima such a big deal? Besides the seeming impossibility of its achievement, the demonstration of love for our enemies would begin to transform the Japanese culture, as their culture holds the victorious in honor but lacks dignity and compassion for those who are conquered.

By loving our enemies, the Japanese people would be able to receive restoration as an act of honor, not just love.[306] As Americans, we do not fully grasp the idea of an honor-based culture and just how deep this sense of honor goes. For Americans who lost loved ones or who were tortured by the Japanese, their greatest healing would come through forgiving the Japanese and restoring them by their love and actions.

When it came to the city of Hiroshima, people thought it would not be able to be rebuilt for seventy years due to the destruction and radiation fallout.[307] The resiliency of the Japanese people proved otherwise. They set out to rebuild the city for "making a strong stand against the city's fate in the bombing, a dream of building a peaceful future, a thorough plan to make a stronger city, seeing the sky so the buildings are kept low, and sacrificing immediate comfort for the benefit of the long-term prosperity of the city."[308] The Japanese did not delay in rebuilding the city but launched the restoration of their infrastructure.

The cost to rebuild did not enter the hearts or minds of the Japanese people. The city's "mission for the future involved a transformation into the city of peace."[309] The ambiance of the city emits tranquility. The restoration of Hiroshima proved that the most lethal destruction the world has known cannot stop the human desire to persevere and create a reputation in the future.

BERLIN

In World War II, the European front experienced horrendous devastation. Even though a nuclear bomb was not used in the European theatre, the bombing campaigns combined with the ground assaults grooved paths of pulverization through the countryside. The fourth city studied for its restoration is Berlin, where standing structures were practically nonexistent when the war was over. After Germany surrendered, the Allies considered abandoning Berlin because of the condition of the city. But the people of Berlin did not give up on their city.

At this point, the atrocities committed by the Nazis against the Jewish people and other ethnic groups within the concentration camps had not been fully realized. After the discovery of the genocide, why rebuild Berlin? This genocide required more than "loving your enemies." Executing six million Germans would only add to the death toll, if a life were taken for a life. The only way through to the future involved forgiveness to the people while holding the Nazi leaders accountable for the genocide and inhumane treatment of more than twenty-five million people. When it came to the people of Berlin, "love covers a multitude of sins."[310] This would certainly be understood in a few short years after World War II when the Berlin Airlift kept the city supplied after the Soviets cut off all land routes in a conflict not yet perceived.

Unlike Hiroshima, Berlin became grounds for a political tug-of-war, with the Soviets occupying the East and the French, British, and American forces occupying the West. The women of Berlin formed the backbone of the rebuilding effort, becoming known as the "rubble women"[311] for the amount of rubble requiring removal from the city. "In all, 60,000 women between 15 and 65 years old received conscription to work on the rubble removal."[312] In many ways, the women took the brunt of the Soviet aggression as their spoils of war and carried the shame of what their people represented, following the exposure of the truth. For them to endure abuse following the war and persevere, these women displayed another side of the German people to overcome and endure for others to have a better future.

The people of Berlin, at least on the western side, found out what true compassion was composed of in care. The Soviet Iron Curtain wanted an iron grip on the entire city of Berlin that lay within the occupied territory of East Germany. The Soviets built a blockade and did not allow any vehicle into the city, and they allowed no one to leave, except by air.

The Berlin Airlift began in 1948, with the American military supplying everything from coal to eggs to the citizens of the city. Even though a shot was not fired, this act ignited the Cold War. The struggle involved logistics rather than bullets and persevered to keep the American, French, and British troops in the city. The city's importance only increased when President Kennedy visited in 1963 and made his famous statement, "I am a Berliner!"[313] He said it in German, of course. The city represented freedom on one side and a new type of fascism on the other in the form of fully implemented communism.

Ultimately, Berlin did not undergo complete restoration for decades. Due to the Cold War, half of the city remained unimproved on the eastern side until after the fall of the Berlin Wall on November 9, 1989. At this point, forty-four years had passed, and another generation would partake of liberty the previous generation had not experienced. Full restoration literally happened in another generation. Parts of the city finally received restoration at the dawn of the new millennium. Was this worth it for the people of Berlin? Absolutely! People love to see a city that represents their history and culture brought back to a place of honor and prosperity.

WHAT ABOUT YOUR CITY?

Without a doubt, God has a heart for cities. Scripture begins with the city of Enoch getting established, and it ends with the "New Jerusalem," a cubed city coming down from heaven.[314] But this does not just mean the old Jerusalem is gone. The term *new,* καινός (*kainos*) in the Greek, can also mean "fresh" or "renewed."[315] This terminology indicates the new can come from the old. How many excavations have revealed ancient structures and foundations below a modern city? From Mexico City to Paris, these structures can be a thousand years old or more. Yet, in God's eyes, this is only a day. Whether the city is Jerusalem or Berlin, God clearly loves the cities, and He loves the people within them even more. The restoration of a city can restore hope to an entire ethnic group or nation just by its restoration, even if it is not as grand or glorious as the ones we've looked at here.

After 9/11, New York City seemed to have a cloud of grief and hopelessness over the destruction of the Twin Towers in Manhattan. Yet the building of Freedom Tower created a rebirth and renewal within the city.[316] Notice the language when it comes to a city being "awake" or "alive." Without question, God wants to see life restored in every way. This has been God's goal since Genesis chapter 3, and it will be His goal until all things are restored in the earth.

How big is our vision? God does not just stop with cities. He goes beyond this to people groups and nations. If God is giving us a heart for something, let us pursue it with all we have.

POINTS TO PONDER

1. Has God given you a vision for your city?
2. Following a natural or man-made tragedy, what would you focus on to initiate restoration?
3. How big is your vision for the future of your city?
4. If this were your city, how long would you persevere to see every block restored or rebuilt in a way that brings dignity and honor to you and your ancestors?

10

RESTORATION OF A NATION

Surely you shall call a nation you do not know,
And nations who do not know you shall run to you.[317]

Just as cities carry a huge significance to God, so do nations. God, speaking through the psalmist, declared, "Ask of me and I will give you the nations for your inheritance and the ends of the earth for your possession."[318] That God would consider the nations as an inheritance indicates how much they are truly valued. From the beginning, humankind was created in the likeness and image of God to take dominion.[319] As the population grew, this was meant to break out in a healthy way. But something happened in the Garden of Eden, changing the scope of who had dominion and how it was implemented.

When we speak of *nations*, we are not just referring to countries with defined borders and their own flag, even though they are a part of this. As we examine the first mention of the word *nation* in the Hebrew Scriptures, the term was used in God's declaration to Abraham: "And I will make you a great nation."[320] The Hebrew word גּוֹי (*gowy*), translated as "nation," comes from a root word meaning "mass or swarm."[321] The word has a connotation toward a family, tribe, or clan, which is why the Septuagint used the word *ethnos*—from which we get "ethnic" and "ethnicity"—to translate the meaning.[322] These same words, *gowy* and *ethnos,* in the Hebrew and Greek translations, respectively, were used in

Psalm 2:8. God desires to see every people group restored to their proper place in His kingdom.

The actual reference for *countries* occurred just prior to the reference for *nation*. In Genesis 10:30, *country* came from the Hebrew word הַר, *har*, meaning "mountain or hill."[323] Thus the reference to *mountain* can refer to countries or governments. The next use comes in Genesis 12:1, when God told Abram to leave his country. The word for *country* here, אֶרֶץ, *erets*, signifies "land, earth, or ground."[324] Thus a people group or country can be tied to a certain land. The first use of the word *kingdom* came in "Genesis 10:10 with the Hebrew word הַמַּמְלָךְ, *mamlakah*, from the root for *king*, also meaning 'reign.'"[325] The combination of all these terms makes up our concept of a country.

Just as the nations meant so much to God in the beginning, they also ravish His heart at the end of the age. Both the ethnic groups and the kingdoms need to be valued. We will have "people from every tongue, tribe, people and nation" making up the kingdom of heaven.[326] John had a revelation of all people groups in heaven. Then John declared, "The kingdom of this world has become the kingdom of our God and of His Christ, and He will reign forever and ever."[327] We can play RISK with God, but He will win every time. He wants us to risk everything to see the nations come to Him.

THE CYCLICAL NATURE OF NATIONS

Thanks to history and Scripture not being completely destroyed or rewritten, we have evidence of what happens to empires and countries. If we just look at the pattern within Scripture, a clear, cyclical nature existed within the Jewish nation from the time of the judges through the kings. Each stage gets added to the next, and the first three are interchangeable or even simultaneous. Let us consider the following list:

1. Apathy
2. Sin/wickedness
3. Apostasy
4. Judgment

5. Repentance
6. Deliverance
7. Order
8. Glory

Apathy does not happen overnight but creeps in slowly, like a frog thrown into a pot of water. By definition, *apathy* is "the absence or suppression of passion, emotion, or excitement; lack of interest in or concern for things that others find moving or exciting."[328] The frog will not jump out of a pot of water if it is slowly being heated to a boil. If the frog were thrown into a pot of boiling water, it would immediately jump out to save its life. Hence, humanity acts very much like the frog in culture. People will not protest if things gradually change. When we consider the dates in the book of Judges, for example, we notice decades fell between different judges needing to be raised up for deliverance as the people repented.

Once people stop having a concern or care, sin and wickedness increase. If people or police as bystanders stop caring to intervene, the depraved population engages in sinful activity, both overtly and covertly. As the consequences decrease, the wickedness increases. Thus apathy increases as well. Prior to the Victorian era in England, thousands of the women engaged in prostitution.[329] William Wilberforce, a British politician who advocated for the abolition of the slave trade at the turn of the nineteenth century, was not only vehemently opposed to slavery; he opposed the depravity of his time and desired to see morality become the "new normal" in culture.[330]

In the presence of sin and wickedness, violence increases as well. After the fall in Genesis 3, a few generations later, in the time of Noah, we witness the report of "violence filling the earth."[331] Then people lose reason and go into apostasy. They see no value in following God. Once people lose their reverence of God, the floodgates open for wickedness and apathy to increase exponentially. If it were not for God intervening, the entire world would implode from the amount of wickedness and violence.

Whether people realize it or not, judgment actually becomes a form of grace. God sits on a throne of grace.[332] The God of the Hebrew Scriptures is the same one in the Greek Scriptures. Plus, God's judgments are "righteous and true."[333] Throughout the time line of the judges and kings, God would either allow Israel's enemies to prevail or would send prophets to proclaim His edict. Sometimes, the judgment God sent was severe. Consider Elijah proclaiming it would not rain, and it did not, for three and a half years.[334] God's judgments remove apathy and give people the ability to awaken their senses spiritually.

Following judgment, repentance can then enter the nation. First, judgment comes on the people who have kept their faith but have still fallen from God's standard.[335] He needs His people to wake up in order to be able to assist others. In God's declaration to Solomon in 2 Chronicles 7, He stated:

> "When I shut up heaven and there is no rain, or command the locusts to devour the land, or send pestilence among my people, if My people who are called by My name will humble themselves, and pray and seek my face, and turn from their wicked ways, then I will hear from heaven, and will forgive their sin and heal their land."[336]

Now people understand why God judges His own followers first. The people of God effect change during a judgment, transforming the condition of the land. The Hebrew word for heal is *rapha*, רָפָא, meaning "heal, cure, or mend."[337] Restoration gets initiated through God's people responding in the midst of judgment or following it.

The declaration of God to Solomon after the dedication of the temple illustrated the concept of repentance. Both humility and repentance go together. We must admit we have missed the mark, which does take humility. God gives His grace to the humble.[338] *Repentance* is "turning from our wicked ways."[339] This means our free will must actively engage in the process. When humility comes upon one person, God can make a difference.[340] When an entire country repents, from the leader to every facet of society, God can even change His mind about judgment before it comes. In the case of Jonah being sent to Nineveh, this happened.[341] Repentance can be initiated by any one of us when we are motivated by love in true humility.

When repentance transforms a nation, a new kind of order gets established. On the occasion of Solomon dedicating the temple, a new order had been brought in following a judgment. Previously, King David had taken a census, which was forbidden without the people giving a ransom, or else a plague would break out.[342] But after the judgment came in the form of a plague, King David bought a piece of property and constructed an altar to the LORD, which, according to tradition, was where the temple was eventually built when King Solomon placed everything in order and built the temple.

Following the proper order, God made Israel prosper. The true prosperity did not come from Solomon's wisdom. A man named Obed-Edom had the Ark of the Covenant at his household for three months, and everything of his was blessed.[343] Thus the glory of God represented true peace, where nothing is missing and all is well. Following the Ark of the Covenant getting placed in the temple, the Israelites witnessed the glory of God coming to the temple and, by location, to the land belonging to Israel.[344] God's desire for every nation is to live in peace and prosperity. Every nation of the world can be somewhere in this cycle.

REQUIREMENTS FOR NATIONAL RESTORATION

God would not leave us hanging without any instructions. God gave increasing levels of discipline to the people if they did not change their ways.[345] In the midst of the cyclical nature of nations, we perceive certain keys emerging. The keys remain with us as His people. In addition to humility and repentance, other factors come into use in establishing and restoring nations.[346] The cyclical nature of nations integrates with some requirements to bring national restoration. Both historically and scripturally, there are four facets to establishing a new foundation:

1. Deliverance
2. Declarations
3. Design/details
4. Divine order

Deliverance is needed, from our enemies or from our own messes. Declarations, both new and old, create our framework for what the results should be. The design or details give us the way of implementing the declarations. If we use the prophetic vision God has delivered or restored to us, then a divine order establishes a restoration that can be permanent.

For our time, some of the greatest keys for restoration are mentioned in the books of Isaiah and Jeremiah. First, let us consider what Isaiah 60 declares:

> Arise, shine; for your light has come, and the glory of the Lord has risen upon you. For behold, darkness will cover the earth and deep darkness the peoples; but the Lord will rise upon you and His glory will appear upon you. Nations will come to your light, and kings to the brightness of your rising. Lift up your eyes round about and see; they all gather together, they come to you. Your sons will come from afar, and your daughters will be carried in the arms. Then you will see and be radiant, and your heart will thrill and rejoice; because the abundance of the sea will be turned to you, the wealth of the nations will come to you.[347]

God's grace comes in His glory rising upon us. Notice that both ethnic groups and leaders will to us. When our culture lies ensnared in deep darkness, our light will penetrate this and draw people out. Our light can be both literal and figurative. The first 120 disciples had literal tongues of fire appear over them.[348] The illumination can also be figurative for understanding, creativity, and designs to set the world free. The wealth comes to finance the answers we develop.

In reading about Jeremiah the prophet, God gave us some other clues. In Jeremiah's calling, God told him, "See, I have appointed you this day over the nations and over the kingdoms, to pluck up and to break down, to destroy and to overthrow, to build and to plant."[349] In a similar manner, we have a similar mandate as Christians.

Through the Great Commission, Jesus ordered us to make disciples of all the nations.[350] In Christ, we become carriers of God's glory and extend the kingdom of God wherever we are. We are called to destroy the works of darkness and overthrow every evil system. It their place, we build according to the pattern God has given us. For us, planting involves sowing the seeds of restoration observable for hundreds of years or longer with God's foundation. If we use His ideas and His patterns, we have something beneficial to the nations and His kingdom work.

Deliverance normally comes after the people cry out. As Jonah proved, judgment does not necessarily need to happen. But God's people can initiate deliverance at any time within a nation, regardless of the stage it is in. God's people are a majority when it is just one person lined up with Him. Just one of us can stand in the gap.[351] God also looks for unity in the deliverance process. In the case of Gideon, he narrowed out the crowd to three hundred so the entire nation of Israel would realize God was the one who brought deliverance, not their might.[352] In the case of the USA, fifty-six men unified as representatives at the beginning to publicly declare independence, with their names inscribed, to initiate deliverance from tyranny.

Declarations on the natural and spiritual levels can set the tone and course for entire countries. Before the USA came into existence, Rev. Robert Hunt planted a cross in the ground as he came upon the North American continent at Cape Henry in 1607 and declared, "The gospel will go forth from these shores, not only to this land, but to all the nations of the earth."[353] Rev. Hunt was not the only settler to make such a declaration. "John Winthrop preached, 'We shall be as a city upon a hill.'"[354] Several people gave declarations by planting a crop of ripe ideas into the foundation of a new nation. Just after the Declaration of Independence, Thomas Paine penned his revolutionary statement, "These are the times that try men's souls."[355] Without question, words have power to tear down as well as build up.

Once the declarations are made, the design and details for what the future holds need to be created. Using the USA as an example, the establishment of a government with a ratified constitution took years. The founding fathers prayed over its development. Members argued over its content. Some details, like the Bill of Rights, needed to be added as amendments. Even though it was not perfect, the US Constitution initiated a form of government giving power to the people.

The design and implementation following a divine order has the best hope because it can last forever—literally. Certain ethnic groups and nations get mentioned throughout Scripture, while others are not specifically mentioned. But God had them all in mind from the foundation of the world. God so loved the world—meaning the entire world system—He gave His only begotten Son, so that none would have to perish but come to everlasting life.[356] God has a divine order for every ethnic group and every country on the planet. People simply need to ask God for His plan to be revealed, along with how to implement it fully.

ISRAEL

As we connect the dots through history, it makes sense to focus on Israel, since we previously examined the city of Jerusalem. Due to biblical prophecy and historical significance, Israel will be our first case study of national restoration.

The restoration of Israel as a country has to be the most significant event in our history since Jesus walked the earth. If we consider the pattern according to Scripture, we can perceive it getting repeated in the recreation of the state of Israel. The tragedy of the Holocaust brought a deliverance of the Jews from around the world to the Promised Land. They cried out to God, and He heard them. Declarations came out to make a place for the Jewish people. But one had been in place for over two millennia.

The Jewish Bible ends with 2 Chronicles 36:23, which states, "Thus says Cyrus king of Persia, 'The Lord, the God of heaven, has given me all the kingdoms of the earth, and He has appointed me to build Him a house in Jerusalem, which is in Judah. Whoever there is among you of all His people, may the Lord his God be with him, and let him go up!'" This decree became a declaration following World War II.

The details for a Jewish state came to fruition, as we've already mentioned, with their own Declaration of Independence issued in May 1948. Not all the details lined up with God's heart, but this was a start. Following the Six-Day War, Israel gained the capital, Jerusalem, the West Bank, the Golan Heights, the Gaza Strip, and the Sanai Peninsula. Fifty years after Israel took Jerusalem, the "Second Cyrus, President Trump," recognized Jerusalem as the official capital of Israel and moved the American embassy there on the seventieth anniversary of Israel as a nation.[357] The timing and significance of both fifty and seventy represented Jubilee and completion, respectively. During Jubilee, the Jewish people had all debts cancelled and received freedom if they had become a slave.[358]

GERMANY

Of all things, God's grace can never be underestimated. Under Hitler and the Nazi regime, Germany executed more than six million Jews along with another twenty million people who didn't fit with their plan and worldview. Germany went from occupying most of Europe in 1942 to being occupied by the Allies after their defeat on May 8, 1945. Germany underwent judgment according to the cyclical nature of a nation.

The German people had to realize their wickedness and have the humility to own it and repent. One of the most famous pictures from this era captured the German soldiers being forced to see a film of a concentration camp after it had been liberated.[359] Some men were covering their faces so they wouldn't be photographed. Others just sat in shock at what they viewed. Many of them had no idea of the horrors their nation had committed, which they were protecting. The grace of God abounds where the sin has been the greatest.[360] The USA was the only nation who suffered little damage and lost fewer lives when compared to other countries involved in the war, and thus they had the capacity to occupy as well as rebuild.

Providentially placed both during and after the war, General George Marshall constructed a plan to care for much of the war-torn areas and to rebuild the nations who suffered. The Marshall Plan gave the details for restoring everyone—including Germany. His plan worked so well, West Germany became one of the strongest economies in the world. Declarations still continued. While standing at the Berlin Wall in 1987, President Ronald Reagan declared, "Mr. Gorbachev, tear down this wall!" Through God's grace and many saints praying, the Iron Curtain fell two years later, and Germany was able to be reunified.

JAPAN

Unlike Germany, Japan suffered a judgment no other nation has. To this date, Japan has been the only nation to have atomic weapons used against it. Many people do not know this, but President Truman saw an atomic attack as the only way to save millions of lives. After the Battle of Iwo Jima and the Battle of Okinawa, American intelligence noted the samurai mentality embedded within their culture would enable the Japanese to fight to the last man, until there were none remaining. The USA had to get Japan to agree to an unconditional surrender—or there would be no more Japan. Hence, the use of atomic warfare displayed a power the Japanese could not withstand. The Japanese agreed to an unconditional surrender aboard the USS *Missouri* on August 14, 1945.

Japan experienced judgment for war crimes and atrocities committed in multiple places. Their worldview had to change, and their emperor was no longer considered a god. Due to their honor-based culture, they had a national shame to overcome, which was tied to the same samurai mentality that enabled them to fight. Following this, Japan experienced grace in ways they were not expecting either. General MacArthur, who understood their worldview, was placed in charge of overseeing the American occupation in Japan. He also invited American missionaries to help in transforming the Japanese worldview, though very few answered the call. However, General MacArthur engaged with the Japanese in such an honorable way that his portrait remains in many houses and buildings to this day.

Japan also received assistance under the Marshall Plan. God's grace came in the form of a businessman from Wyoming. William Edwards Deming assisted the Japanese manufacturing industry in getting jump-started. Mr. Deming had this new idea called "quality control" to ensure manufactured products came out with the exact specifications to make them more reliable to work. For its small size, Japan became the number two economy in the world because of Mr. Deming's ideas put into practice. To this day, one of the highest awards given in Japan is called "The Deming Prize," which is awarded to the people adding to the area of quality control and "total quality management."[361] Japanese products are still known for their reliability in the modern marketplace.

THE UNITED STATES

If anything should give us hope, the Marshall Plan is a great example. We've described just a bit of how, through the Marshall Plan, the USA helped restore and establish Japan, Germany, Israel, and many other nations following World War II. Prior to this, the USA assisted the nations following World War I. As a nation, we "must not grow weary in doing good, for in due time we will reap if we do not grow weary."[362] We will reap what we have sown. We have the law of sowing and reaping, or seedtime and harvest, which continues through the natural seasons as well as the spiritual seasons.[363] This nation has gone through its cycles, but God's plans are just beginning to unfold.

Considering the cycle of nations, the USA has passed through the different stages of discipline more than once. The New Madrid earthquakes in 1811–12, followed soon after by the War of 1812, tested the new republic. The cholera pandemic that broke out in 1846 was devastating. The Civil War revealed the compromise of the *US Constitution*, in that it allowed slavery and considered a slave only three-fifths of a person. This language remained completely contrary to *The Declaration of Independence*, which declared that all men are created equal by their Creator, with certain unalienable rights, being life, liberty, and the pursuit of happiness.

The Spanish flu came at the tail end of World War I in 1918; it wiped out 5 percent of the world's population and killed more Americans in one year than all of World War I.[364] The Great Depression and the drought through the 1930s tested American resolve once again. Then World War II followed. The Korean War broke out in 1950, followed by the Vietnam War shortly thereafter, in 1955.

Communism was introduced within the academic community of the USA, along with the Kinsey Report, which advocated sexual behavior in all forms, leading to the sexual revolution. Both communism and the Kinsey literature unleashed destruction continuing into the current era. On a spiritual level, prayer was removed from schools in 1962. All of academics went completely secular and embraced the communist worldview. Abortion was legalized in 1973. Apostasy set in. Then 9/11 happened. Was this judgment or a wake-up call? The USA has been involved in conflicts since then. Then the year 2020 came.

THE COVID CONDITION

I thought 9/11 took the wrong response, and travel has not been the same since. I hope someone did not make a one-dollar bet and say they could make it even worse. COVID-19 and the resulting panic led to a world shutdown and lockdown, keeping everyone isolated. World economies caught a cold in 2020. Entire nations shut down everything. The only thing not shut down in the USA in 2020 were riots ruining the businesses that could not even open. What is the endgame? The darkest time comes right before the dawn.

God has details He is working out. We are in a place where the enemy ultimately is spiritual but using physical puppets. Jesus told us to be of good cheer because He has overcome the world.[365] We are called to be overcomers, and we are here for such a time as this! Where the enemy has come in, like a flood the Spirit of God has come rushing in.[366]

More prayer and repentance has gone out in this time than ever before. In the midst of the COVID condition, Lou Engle and 72,000 Christians fasted and prayed for forty days. Abraham, as one man, convinced God to spare Sodom and Gomorrah on the basis of ten righteous people, but there were not even ten to be counted. We have much more than Abraham crying out in these times. The best cure for the COVID condition is shutting off the media and social media. We must become producers rather than consumers. We can produce powerful prayers, uplifting content, joyful fellowship, and love our neighbor as ourselves. God has saved His best wine for last, not just for a wedding but for the USA and the entire world.

COLD WAR II

The COVID condition has led to Cold War II. The only major difference happens to be that the dragon (China) is at the forefront, rather than the bear (Russia). Iran is undermining American efforts throughout the Middle East and is set on the destruction of Israel. North Korea seems to do a bait-and-switch tactic. The European Union continually works to push an agenda involving fear and control with open migration. The war is "cold" because the enemies are within and without.

Is there a way out? We have the open door before us that no one can shut because of God working.[367] In nations like China, Russia, North Korea, and Iran, the underground churches are thriving and expanding so fast, no one knows exactly how large the population is. Let us seek God to "perceive what He is up to and join Him in it."[368] God wants a "hot war" where people are burning with the fire of His love. This is already breaking out. Many rioters lit all kinds of destructive fires in the natural. But we have the fire of the Holy Spirit, and we will not quench the fire He has placed within us. It is our turn to go light the fires and see who will be set ablaze.

SHEEP NATIONS RISING

These are the most exciting days to be alive! We are witnessing the greatest travail and transformation the world has ever observed. The Lord has entrusted us to be a part of what He is doing in the earth. For any of us who are in Christ, we clearly have a purpose to be alive, placed in our respective nations to see the kingdom of God expanded in the earth. Paul stated, "And He has made from one blood every nation of mankind to live on all the face of the earth, having determined their appointed times and the boundaries of their habitation."[369] We have been placed into our assignment at this time, and we do not want to waste this opportunity.

Jesus declared, both before and after His crucifixion, that nations had an opportunity to be a part of His kingdom. Jesus said, "All the nations will be gathered before Him and He will separate them from one another, as the shepherd separates the sheep from the goats."[370] The amazing factor in all of this involves the transforming power of the gospel. "Nothing is impossible with God."[371] God can turn a goat nation into a sheep nation with the assistance of His disciples.

At the conclusion of his gospel, Matthew inscribed the Great Commission, which states, "As you are going, make disciples of *all the nations*, baptizing them in the name of the Father, and of the Son, and of the Holy Spirit, teaching them to observe all that I commanded you."[372] I went through the Greek text to break this down, and this verse contains three participles, with the main verb being "make disciples." The first participle, *going,* could indicate "as we are going through life," meaning we are *on mission* to make disciples right where we are. The other two participles are *teaching* and *baptizing,* signifying practices that should be ongoing.

All is still *all* in the Greek, and *nations* refers to ethnic groups. Therefore, the various ethnic groups within a given country can be a sheep nation. God desires all the nations to be the inheritance of the Lord.[373] How much restoration needs to occur? God truly wants "the restoration of all things."[374] He has called us to partner with Him in this endeavor.

We all have a part to play in the restoration process. According to Malachi, the restoration starts with the family.[375] This gives us a starting point. When one person changes in a family, an entire family system can be transformed. But as Os Hillman says, "There are seven mountains of influence involving family, government, art and entertainment, media, business, education, and religion ("church," as a Christian) to take in order to transform a nation."[376] We must all find our role to play and ask the Lord which mountain He wants us to take. We can even be called to more than one, depending on our abilities or our position. As a father and a chaplain, I am within the family, the church, and the government simultaneously. Like Caleb, we must cry out, "Give me my mountain!"[377] We are all called to participate in some way. We have so much to restore with Him.

Are we ready for the greatest adventure of our lives? Let us find out where God wants us to restore and join Him in the process.

POINTS TO PONDER

1. Are you called to fill the gap somewhere for your nation?
2. What stage in the cycle of nations do you see us in now?
3. How much restoration needs to occur in our nation?
4. What mountain(s) are we called to in order to transform the nation?
5. Are we ready for the greatest adventure of our lives?

11

THE RESTORATION REFORMATION

> "On that day I will raise up the tabernacle of David, which has fallen down, and repair its damages; I will raise up its ruins, and rebuild it as in the days of old; that they may possess the remnant of Edom, and all the Gentiles who are called by My name," says the LORD who does this thing.[378]

Within our Christian spheres of influence, have you wondered why we seem to be behind the culture? From the beginning of this book, I shared how there are programs on restoring houses, cars, and furniture. I would even say that certain programs dealing with people's talents are restoring their respective hopes, dreams, and destinies that have been set aside or lost. And if people wonder why I repeat certain points, it's because I know that learning occurs with repetition. I want the body of Christ to grasp this concept that is so precious to the heart of God. Consider the first definition of a paradox again: "a statement or proposition that seems self-contradictory or absurd but in reality expresses a possible truth."[379] So, what do we do if our culture may actually be prophesying truth in restoration?

Just over five hundred years ago, a reformation occurred within Christendom that shook the foundation of the European church structure. Martin Luther wrote his Ninety-Five Theses to refute the abuses and heresies of his day that existed within the church. He nailed the theses to the door of the church he oversaw as a protest to the status quo of his time, hoping the points would generate discussion. October 31, the day he took this stance, is called Reformation Day and is celebrated annually in Europe because so many people groups experienced a new level of freedom because of his courage.

Ultimately, this Reformation period accelerated the Renaissance period (*renaissance* meaning "rebirth" in French), unleashing art, education, discovery, and innovation throughout Europe. What would happen in the wake of a "Restoration Reformation" within Christendom in our present age? History would record the results of restoration being integrated into the foundation of the church, not just the culture. In order for a reformation to be ignited, certain theses must be mounted on the proverbial door once again but in the areas of religion, education, and government, for starters. These theses would involve the principles required, the people empowered to implement this, and the places set aside to establish the reformation within communities or regions.

THE SEVEN PRIMARY PRINCIPLES

Due to the number of Scriptures that deal with restoration, I had to be intentional in what I highlighted in each chapter. We have established that restoration is the heartbeat of God, so why is it not happening on a regular and systematic basis? We first need common principles of restoration so that everyone can practice them as well as reproduce them wherever a restoration center is established. From the various passages that I have studied, the following seven principles—repentance, repercussions, redirection, renewal, refirement, restoration, and repetition—are the basics that everyone should implement.

Repentance

Without true repentance, there cannot be true restoration. The first principle of repentance restored David but rejected Saul. Saul used excuses when he was confronted by the prophet Samuel.[380] When David was confronted by the prophet Nathan, he stated, "I have sinned against the LORD."[381] David did not blame-shift, that Christian BS. Blame-shifting does not own the failure. Only personal ownership of failure opens up the door of grace. To be philosophical, what if Adam had admitted he failed in the garden rather than shifting the blame to Eve or, ultimately, God? More than likely, there would have been consequences, but perhaps the curses would not have been as harsh. David still had consequences, but the restoration process began with his confession and true repentance.[382]

Repercussions

Without a doubt, sin does have consequences. The second principle is *repercussions*. Paul even declared, "The wages of sin is death."[383] Can we be thankful God's response is not this physically drastic every time we sin? However, as I just referenced in the case of Saul and David, the repercussions for sin become more severe if the person does not repent or if they have failed in the same area more than once. If this were placed in modern terms, a person can be released on parole after the first convicted offense and have freedom to act within the boundaries that are given. Notice that King David did not repeat the offense of adultery ever again in his lifetime. If a person fails in the same area more than once, then the repercussions must be more severe. The person can still be restored, but the repercussions must hurt enough for the person to want to change the behavior as well as the attitude of the heart.

Redirection

Depending on the person and the circumstances, the person who has entered a restoration process might have to go through a phase of *redirection*—the third principle. In the case of John Mark, Paul would have nothing to do with his restoration at the time Barnabas was willing to restore him. Due to the steepness of the disagreement, Barnabas had to leave Paul and take John Mark another way.[384] Several years later, Paul realized the value of the restoration for John Mark, but the principle of redirection was necessary at the time Barnabas felt inspired to carry it out. As I shared in the case of Rev. Jim Bakker, he had to be redirected to a different place and start out in another way by people who had not overseen him before. At the time of this writing, Rev. Bakker has not only received credibility on how many times he has been right but also has influenced others concerning restoration and revelation on an international level once again.

Renewal

In order for anyone to get on the path of restoration, the void must be filled that caused the condition in the first place—hence the fourth principle, *renewal*. Peter proclaimed, "Repent, therefore and return, that your sins may be wiped away, in order that times of refreshing may come from the presence of the Lord."[385] True repentance must always precede renewal. Once repentance has truly occurred, a renewal of the whole person, including the spirit, soul, and body, can begin. That is how any person must come to love God and love others.[386] Renewal integrates the person back into true fellowship with God and gives them a new sense of self-awareness. They become sensitized to the presence and voice of God in every moment. These people act on their own will, but other people come alongside them in order to affirm, confirm, direct, and impart what the Holy Spirit reveals is lacking in the person's life.

Renewal is a process. God desires His relationship with us more than we may ever realize. I am thankful for the "Toronto Blessing" that brought this reality to my life.[387] The concept of "soaking prayer" came from the Toronto Airport Church so people could be filled up and refilled with the Holy Spirit. We are commanded to "keep being filled" with the Holy Spirit.[388] Anyone can run dry, stop, or crash, just like a car suddenly running out of fuel. Some people must relearn their own signs of when their tank is running low. And if a person has been "broken down," another person qualified in "repairs" must come and examine them. Even a car running well needs gas, an oil change, and preventive maintenance. People are not any different when it comes to renewal.

★ *Refirement* (instead of mere retirement)

When I have had the opportunity to be a part of someone's retirement within the military, I have prayed the retiree experiences "re-fire-ment" following their retirement. *Refirement* is the fifth primary principle. I have prayed this same prayer of refirement over people who made a bad decision leading to removal from ministry or official duties but had a heart of repentance and embraced a restoration process.

Even if a person does not commit blatant sin but becomes halfhearted or complacent in their calling, a re-ignition must take place. When Paul wrote to Timothy, he encouraged him to "rekindle afresh the gift of God."[389] Once in a while, someone may accomplish this on their own, but the refirement principle also takes some outside assistance and revelation. "Every matter is confirmed by the testimony of two or three witnesses."[390] Even if a person has their own calling revealed personally by God, having that extra voice confirming the calling enables it to be established.

Restoration

The sixth primary principle involves being properly reset, simply referred to as *restoration*. Restoration is referring to the final touches, indicating all is complete and set back in order. When it comes to a person, this includes position, authority, influence, health, and financial well-being. As a reminder from the second chapter, the Hebrew word שָׁלֹם, *shalom*, means "whole, perfect, just (as in weight)."[391] And, as resonates with me every time I read it, the better translation would be "nothing missing, nothing broken." Restoration is actually this idea of *shalom* in every area where there has been something missing or broken.

When I heard the announcement that a former pastor caught up in pornography was serving again as a janitor, I was in disbelief that this was considered restoration. I have focused on Rev. Bakker because his example is a model for the body of Christ, especially in Western culture. We can see this with a car, house, or antique, so why not a person? God never gives up on anyone. If this is God's heartbeat, then it must be ours as well.

Repetition

Why would *repetition* even be on this list? As a seventh primary principle, some people may not need to go through a repetition. If someone has been restored and fails again, however, God is not done with that person. Once again, if we are the ones who are "spiritual," then we ought to be in the restoration business.[392] We are also instructed in Proverbs 24 that if a righteous person falls seven times, he rises again.[393] This does not merely refer to repentance. *Repentance* was not a term at the time Proverbs was recorded. Historically, one could see a person falling down and getting back up into a proper stance. On the other hand, the audience may consider when a building or wall collapses and must be raised up again.

If repentance provides a scenario where a person may fall seven times and rise again, the area of forgiveness was taken infinitely further by Jesus. He told Peter to forgive seventy times seven.[394] If this were our own child caught in the trespass, we would do whatever it took to get that child back into proper placement and functioning again. The same can be said for God's kids. God is willing to do whatever it takes to see any person fully restored, again and again.

PROCESS OF RESTORATION

The principles of restoration line up with the process of restoration, but there are some differences. Let us take a look at the definition of each. A *principle* is "a fundamental truth or proposition that serves as the foundation for a system of belief or behavior or for a chain of reasoning."[395] A *process* is "a systematic series of actions directed to some end or a continuous action, operation, or series of changes taking place in a definite manner."[396] Therefore, the process is used to adhere to the given set of principles. We shall look at each process used in the restoration principles.

Acknowledgment

If any of us repents, another person must be there to acknowledge the repentance. This is why we are told to "confess our sins to one another and pray for one another, that we may be healed."[397] The Greek word for *heal* is ἰάομαι (*iaomai*), which can also mean "make whole."[398] So we have another word referring to the idea of *shalom* or *restoration*. If we hide our sin, it always creeps back up, but if we tell someone else on this earth, the light or exposure removes the temptation, and there is an admission to receive the help and healing. So, repentance is the principle, but acknowledgment is the process that opens the door for restoration.

Counseling

When we hear this term, we can immediately think of professional counselors, which may be needed in many cases. In order for the principles of repercussions and redirection to be understood by the one entering the restoration process, they need a truth teller to be genuine. As a chaplain, I have been able to witness truth change a person's heart and allow these principles to take hold.

For any of us, the pain of change has to be less than that of staying the same, or we will not endure the process. If we are told the repercussions of remaining where we are, we will be much more willing to get out of that rut and not go back. The prophet Nathan gave David counseling and laid out the repercussions. Through this, David was able to be redirected and eventually restored. If we look over the rest of David's life, he did not take another wife or have inappropriate relations with any other woman after the incident with Bathsheba. David changed because of the counseling he received.

Character

God wants the very best for all of us. Every one of us has gifts, abilities, and assignments placed by God, and no one can change this.[399] Gifts are given, talents are stewarded, and fruit is grown. When it comes to the fruit of the Spirit, we must cultivate this fruit, or it will not produce.[400] I find it very interesting; the fruit of the Spirit is listed just prior to Paul's challenge to the "spiritual" people to restore.[401] God is so interested in our character, He will do whatever it takes to get us transformed.

Even before Jesus died on the cross, the very nature and character of individuals could be changed by God. In some cases, God even changed their name! *Jacob* means "deceiver or supplanter," but God changed his name to *Israel*, meaning "God prevails, or soldier of God."[402] Even if some people have a bad name, God has a way of transforming someone to not live up to that name. In the case of Jabez, his name means "he causes pain."[403] Yet character matters. Jabez "was more honorable than his brothers."[404] Even though his name indicated harm, his honor reflected his character. God listened to Jabez and answered his prayer by blessing him and not allowing him to cause pain or have pain.[405] Redeeming a name has as much impact as changing a name. Jabez cried out for a transformation, and he received it.

Observation

When someone is caught doing something wrong, they are not simply released and given free rein. When my dad went through treatment for alcoholism, he was kept in the rehabilitation center for six months to ensure he did not sneak anything on anyone. This included not using shaving cream with alcohol in it because the staff had seen patients filter it out and drink it in the past. People need about a month to form a new habit. My clinical pastoral education supervisor, W. Dean Dyk, stated, "The best indicator for future behavior is past performance."[406] Observation time serves as an indicator of how the restoration process is taking hold and the individual is forming new habits.

Depending on the severity and repetition of the moral or ethical failure, the observation time may have to be longer. A unique aspect of humanity comes in the form of our differences. No two people have the same attributes or motivations. Some people can quit drinking alcohol, if it has been an issue, over a heartfelt conviction and not ever touch a drop again. Others must have restraints placed on them and go through a detoxification that lasts several months. Just one issue has a number of different variables. Within this observation time, accountability sets in to God, to the person alongside them, to the respective community, and to themselves.

Understanding

Out of numerous principles in Western civilization, the art has been lost when it comes to understanding. When Jesus explained the parable of the sower, He stated, "But he who received seed on the good ground is he who hears the word and understands it, who indeed bears fruit and produces."[407] Both a counselor and their client need a mutual understanding, but the person undergoing the restoration must grasp the failure, the grace being extended, and the opportunity.

For many people, patient endurance does not develop enough for the client to understand all of the aspects and thus undergo the full restoration process. For this reason, each client cannot be given an automatic timetable for the length of the restoration. Some people are quick to repent. Others have an easier time grasping concepts or ideas and applying them to their lives. Some people are willing to submit more than others. All of these factors make a difference.

Narrative

When it comes to understanding, many people have not perceived their own narrative. People must analyze their own life story and then place it on a schematic where God's narrative has already been laid out. When multiple layers exist to the blueprints, people can lose sight of how many phases go into a building project when only the electrical set is viewed or maybe the plumbing. God's set of blueprints encompasses everything. God knows what went into the person's childhood, what the parents were like, when the first triumph took place, and when mistakes were made. God does not keep track to punish but to build and rebuild the individual. A client must view God's narrative as an active project every day. The Master Builder does not make mistakes, and His finished product gets the most attention.

Training

Nothing replaces training in a new field or culture. All sports have training camps. All military branches have basic training. Numerous trades and businesses have an apprenticeship or a training phase, regardless of the person's education or experience. When it comes to restoration, people need the same basic training. Muscle memory needs to be formed. New habits need to be built. New neural pathways must be laid down to replace the old ones.

Depending on the healing and rebuilding that is required, the training could be for a longer time. A neurosurgeon goes through twelve years of residency beyond medical school. I am just saying … Depending on what the restoration process relates to, training could make all the difference. "To whom much is given, that much more may be required."[408] An electrician apprentice must undergo the process for four years before becoming a full journeyman. I would not want someone to die because of getting hooked into the wrong power grid at the wrong time.

People with an anointing and a destiny must be properly aligned and equipped. This means these people require trainers who have a heart to see the finished product in the form of a person. The clients need trustworthy vessels they can share their innocence with from beginning to end.

PARACLETE PEOPLE

In order for the principles and process to be lived out as a practice, people must clearly be involved. God will still do his part, but the body of Christ is supposed to practice restoration like a doctor practices medicine. Paul said the spiritual people would be the ones to restore members who have fallen.[409] I mentioned the need for these Paraclete People in chapter 6, but their importance in the process of restoration is crucial. The Holy Spirit is the Paraclete, as one who comes alongside us to help, and Paraclete People come alongside the person needing restoration as a partner with the Holy Spirit.[410] As representatives of the Holy Spirit, they must be held to a high standard since they are dealing with souls in a broken and vulnerable position. These people must have certain characteristics in order to be involved. After studying carefully, I believe the following traits should reside in each Paraclete Person.

Credibility

Since coming alongside others is a unique calling to a type of ministry, the Scriptures show us that certain credentials resided within all the people who were called. At the forefront, these Paraclete People must have credibility—and not just perceived credibility. When it came to choosing people to serve tables, like Stephen, they chose him because he was "full of faith and the Holy Spirit."[411] Just think what the ramifications are for serving the restoration of people! The level of trust required for a person's soul cannot be understated or underestimated. These Paraclete People must be held to the standard of an overseer because they are overseeing the restoration of a member to the body of Christ. This does include both men and women. We need the father heart of God as well as the mother heart of God in redeeming an individual.

Passion for People

After credibility, Paraclete People not only need a passion for Jesus but also a passion for people to be restored and to fulfill their destiny in God. This will not be a place for a career but a place for people called to serve at a capacity requiring all of their talents and treasure. Having worked as a chaplain for years, I can tell you that caring for people's souls can be exhausting work. However, soul care can be one of the most rewarding and fulfilling callings in a person's life.

Spiritual

What does it mean to be spiritual? Paul's commandment for restoration was to those who were "spiritual."[412] Unlike many other places where that word comes from the Greek for *charisma*, this Greek word is actually πνεύματι (*pneumati*), which is the dative form meaning "of the spirit."[413] This indicates how they are acting or the means by which they are acting. The use of the term indicates they will act in a way opposite of the flesh or of how humanity sees and does things. Rather, Paraclete People literally are of the Holy Spirit. They are His instruments within the restoration process. Obviously, in a Christian context and a Christian process, the people working with others must be Christians who have an indwelling of the Holy Spirit. In reference back to Stephen, these people are full of faith and the Holy Spirit.[414] These people will stand out among their peers.

Gentleness

Restoration must have been significant in Paul's day, or he would not have added this much detail within this short of a space. He described how this spirituality should be done, "in a spirit of gentleness."[415] The Greek word is πραότητος (*prautetos*), which means "gentleness, humility, and meekness."[416] Jesus used this same root word when He described Himself.

In other words, as people moved by the Holy Spirit, we are to be Christlike in how we act and treat others. This is not with a whip, like with the money changers, but like the shepherd using his staff to guide the sheep a different way. He did not condemn them; He redeemed them. *Meekness* is strength under control. His strength in us must be bridled in order to care for His bride, the church.

Mature

If Paraclete People are going to be like Christ and walk in the Spirit, then they are going to be mature in their faith. This does not reference age but spiritual growth. In the natural, people go through growth spurts—some more exceptional than others. Some friends of ours have a son who is over seven feet tall at age seventeen. If some people grow faster than others in the natural, than some people will grow faster than others in spiritual things too. In the qualifications for ministry, Paul said they should "not be a novice."[417] Paraclete People are not completely new to the faith; they are people who grasp the ways of God well and follow through with them in their own life. Paul described mature Christian behavior in the context of restoration in his letter to the Galatians, stating this:

> Brothers *and sisters*, even if a person is caught in any wrongdoing, you who are spiritual are to restore such a person in a spirit of gentleness; *each one* looking to yourself, so that you are not tempted as well. Bear one another's burdens, and thereby fulfill the law of Christ. For if anyone thinks that he is something when he is nothing, he deceives himself. But each one must examine his own work, and then he will have *reason for* boasting, *but* to himself alone, and not to another. For each one will bear his own load. The one who is taught the word is to share all good things with the one who teaches *him*. Do not be deceived, God is not mocked; for whatever a person sows, this he will also reap. For the one who sows to his own flesh will reap destruction from the flesh, but the one who sows to the Spirit will reap eternal life from

the Spirit. Let's not become discouraged in doing good, for in due time we will reap, if we do not become weary. So then, while we have opportunity, let's do good to all people, and especially to those who are of the household of the faith.[418]

Paul desired Paraclete People as well.

Willingness

As I mentioned before, partnering with people is not a position for someone seeking merely to have a good career. Paraclete People can make a living doing this, but the paycheck cannot be the motivation. Paraclete People are called to be restorers, willing to help others as if they were ministering to the Lord Himself. Due to their calling and their willingness, they must be paid their proper wages. People must keep the proper perspective of a calling rather than a career. Paul made a case for this as well. "Elders do not serve at their own expense and an ox is not muzzled while it treads out the grain."[419] Since Paraclete People are caring for souls, they frequently do not have time to go out and do their own personal fundraising. They are not meant to take a meager salary either, for the sake of the "ministry." Paraclete People must be taken care of because of their willingness to serve in the restoration of valuable members of the body of Christ.

Consistent

Paraclete People must be consistent in their life. In all the traits mentioned, they must maintain their relationship with God, as well as their faith, character, health, families, finances, and home. Paraclete People must remain consistent in their treatment of clients and of colleagues. They will need to be intentional in all these ways. In order to remain consistent, proper rest and self-care must be given and taken. People who work in oncology take vacations, both short and extended. The doctors and nurses I have worked with took a week off every quarter and an extended three-week vacation at least once a year in order to stay healthy. Rest becomes a weapon in their arsenal. Paraclete People have the greatest goal and greatest reward of restoring people to their place in the body of Christ. All of us need them to be consistent in restoring wholeness and remaining in it for as long as the calling keeps them.

Prescriptive Places

Having grown up in open country, I find in my life that <u>certain places just bring renewal and refreshment to the soul.</u> People who have climbed to ten thousand feet to stand on the edge of an emerald-green lake full of golden cutthroat trout with ripe raspberries to pick and eat all around can appreciate such a place. In God, certain places had an extra special touch that meant something to Him. When Jacob fled, he "happened to" lie down at a place where he saw a ladder ascending into heaven, with angels going up and down.[420] Anyone would notice the place was special. Jacob said that very place was "the house of God and the gate of heaven."[421] God revealed the significance of this place to Jacob (meaning "deceiver") after he had stolen Esau's blessing. God has a way of getting us to a right place with Him after we commit an offense.

Cities of Refuge

Within Hebrew Scriptures, people had an opportunity to run to a place established by God in case they found themselves caught in a trespass involving someone's life. These "cities of refuge" had a placement and disbursement throughout the kingdom, allowing everyone an opportunity to run to a place to escape the death penalty.[422] Prior to the cross of Christ, God still revealed His heart in wanting people to have an opportunity for justice and redemption. At this point in time, it was the only option for a person who killed someone. These people were offered a reset and a ransom for their life to be redeemed.

Modern cities of refuge are required in our current culture, not just for the killer but for those broken off from the body of Christ. Even though all sin is sin, certain categories come with a stigma attached to them. In certain movements, if a minister is divorced, even if the divorce is not his fault, he loses his ordination and his opportunity to ever serve again in ministry. Due to an oversexualized culture, there is no shortage of sexual sin, which also comes with a stigma. Or what if someone steals from the church tithes and offerings fund? We could go through an entire list of sins, but the command remains the same. "If a person is caught in *any* trespass," they must be given the opportunity to receive total restoration.[423]

Places of Restoration

God restored people, property, kingdoms and callings at certain places. In some cases, cities of refuge doubled as a place for restoration. In the case of King David, the kingdom was restored to him at Hebron, one of the cities of refuge.[424] Just as the cities of refuge had significance for why they were chosen, places around the world are conducive to restoring people to their first love and confirming their purpose. Perhaps you have a place on your heart where a restoration center would be ideal. Certain ministries and nonprofit organizations work in inner healing or wholeness for people. Some nonprofit organizations are not specifically Christian but work on restoring people rescued out of the sex-trafficking industry. The Paraclete People who have a heart for this may have a part to play in picking and establishing the places optimal for the restoration process to be facilitated.

LAUNCHING A LEGACY

In order to inaugurate a Restoration Reformation, the right people and the appropriate resources are needed to establish this Christian principle for the long haul. The body of Christ does not need another fad but must undergo a transformation where restoration is an aspect of church culture throughout the world. I do not have the resources to establish every place and pay every person's salary, but "we have the mind of Christ."[425] Together, we can take the blueprints and run with it. This is a legacy for the body of Christ that needs to be carried on to usher in the King of kings. After all, "the restoration of all things" must take place before He comes.[426]

The church must work together in unity for the common goal of seeing restoration take place around the globe. In the wake of COVID-19, many people are seeing the need for economic and social restoration. But people are the most highly valued commodity in God's eyes because we were created in the likeness and image of God, with a living soul.[427] God's purpose involves humanity carrying out His intent throughout all the earth. His great story begins and ends with restoration woven all the way in between the pages of Scripture and history. Now is the time for us to see this legacy launched.

Points to Ponder

1. How many principles of restoration have you observed or practiced?
2. How would you implement a process of restoration?
3. Who would you set as Paraclete People to oversee restoration?
4. What special places are you aware of that would be prescriptive for God to work?
5. What would it take to launch a legacy of restoration?

12

WHERE DO WE GO FROM HERE?

"So I will restore to you the years that the swarming locust has eaten, the crawling locust, the consuming locust, and the chewing locust, My great army which I sent among you. You shall eat in plenty and be satisfied, and praise the name of the LORD your God, who has dealt wondrously with you; and My people shall never be put to shame."[428]

Why does it have to be so hard to get to the point of launch? No matter what the scenario, this is never easy to do. Thanks to the space age in which we live, launching does make a great metaphor for the different facets of our lives. The context of the effort does not make a difference, whether it is launching a business, patenting a new invention, or releasing a new product. Adding to this difficulty, a visionary who sees things that the "normal" person cannot even conceive may fight an uphill battle throughout their life span.

The people who know us best can be our biggest critics. As I shared the story of Joseph's life, his family could not see what God had revealed to him. This may not always be the case, but family and friends can be a huge hindrance because, as close as they are, the vision that lies within you may not fit the mold that they may have constructed for you. This can include your church family or faith community. They would like to keep you where you are, no matter what it takes. How many times has someone tried to keep you in a box that they have built for you and your life?

As if this was not enough to overcome, the process of restoring our own vision, project, business, book, or ministry can seem daunting, especially if it has been destroyed completely. Take Joseph, for example; the dreams he expressed toward the end of his life were not going to be fulfilled in his lifetime.[429] He knew that his people had to go back to the land that was promised to them through Abraham, which he did not even see in his lifetime, but he perceived an eternal perspective when it came to God fulfilling His promises. Even if we do not see the ultimate restoration in our lifetime, we must pursue it with all that we have, as if it depends on us in our generation.

THE CASE OF BILLY MITCHELL

During my time serving in the air force, one common name everyone learns is Billy Mitchell, who earned the unlikely title as "prophet of the Air Force."[430] This was not his own title, but the title of his critics, which has turned out to be a term of endearment in the present. Like a prophet, Billy Mitchell was a true visionary. He served under Major General John J. Pershing during World War I as a member of the Army Signal Corps, which is what the airplanes of the time fell under. The term *air force* had not come into being yet. However, Mitchell's experience with the use of air power in the form of reconnaissance, strategic bombing, and air support for ground troops shaped his vision and produced a drive in him to prove that air power was the wave of the future.

Following World War I, Mitchell began to prove his theories of air power. The most famous demonstration of his proof came on July 21, 1921, when he had planes sink a captured German battleship from the Great War, the *Ostrfriesland*, "with one direct hit from a bomb dropped by an airplane, fulfilling his own prophecy that a plane could sink a battleship."[431] This act, however, did not earn him friendship; rather, it gained him enemies in military circles, especially in the form of the chief of naval operations. Up to this point in thousands of years of recorded history, the two distinguishing aspects of a military superpower were its standing army and the size of its navy. A paradigm shift had providentially taken place. The political backlash from Mitchell's demonstration resulted in his court-martial hearing in 1925.[432]

For anyone who has been in the military, a person who makes the general ranks is typically a triple type A personality, or what one would consider a very high D (dominant) on the DiSC profile. Mitchell would have come across as arrogant, especially after stating that planes would go faster than the speed of sound, which earned him mockery from every angle.[433] There is no question that he was a visionary who seemed to have been born in the wrong time period. Statements like this from Mitchell are the reason this trial and story made it into a Hollywood script, *The Court-Martial of Billy Mitchell.*[434]

As the case of Billy Mitchell illustrated, no one understood what he did when he was placed under trial in 1925.[435] Everyone thought he was crazy because he foresaw air superiority as the wave of the future.[436] Mitchell advocated for a separate air force following his military career but did not see it come to fruition in his lifetime. He passed away in 1936, but the dream and the vision Mitchell possessed did not.

Following the enormous expense and effort of World War II, air power proved its usefulness and advantage on all sides. Mitchell's dream of a separate air force was born through the National Defense Authorization Act of 1947.[437] Even though Mitchell was not alive to see his dream come true, some of his critics were alive to see many things he perceived come to pass. Soon after the establishment of the United States Air Force in September 1947, Chuck Yeager broke the sound barrier in the Bell X-1 rocket plane the following month.[438] Billy Mitchell, even after his death, was vindicated for all time.

HIT THE RESET BUTTON

Remarkably, throughout Scripture and history, numerous people, cities, and nations initiated a reset that resulted in a restoration within their lifetime and generation. Having grown up with electronic games, I always liked the reset button feature where the whole game could be launched with a fresh start. That is exactly what we have been given through Christ. Jesus paid the price for our false start in the Garden of Eden in Genesis 3.

Ever since Jesus died on the cross nearly two thousand years ago, an entire reset occurred that has forever shifted humanity and the entire cosmos on a different course.

Perhaps you are like me, where your life was on the wrong trajectory, but God set it straight. This reset button has happened in my life more than once. The first reset happened when I was president of a fraternity in college, when a Vietnam veteran named Ed led me to a whole new life and way of thinking. Another reset happened when I was told that I would not be qualified for ministry because of having a different view from the leadership at the time. The Lord saw that differently as well, where a number of key people in my life helped with the reset in my life. This reset took a few years but was absolutely worth the time, preparation, and character building. In my current role, God has allowed many dreams, visions, and prophecies to be fulfilled, and the journey is not over yet!

Thanks to living in Hail Alley as well as Tornado Alley, I have seen entire communities devastated within fifteen minutes. Depending on the devastation, the rebuilding can take anywhere from one to five years. As I shared earlier, both Jerusalem and Berlin took intentionality, time, and determination to see the rebuilding completed. Some natives to the area would say that the restoration is a continual process. However, the time the reset button is hit can also be known as a point of demarcation.

As a nation, Israel saw this point of demarcation when President Truman recognized the restored nation of Israel in 1948. Some resets are much larger than others, but the point is pursuit. From the individual to the community to the nation, restoration is the ultimate goal following any type of loss or devastation. Depending on the sacrifice required, the reward to see restoration come to pass can mean the fulfillment of a lifetime.

Make Time to Seek the Original Author

As I pointed out in the second chapter, restoration is clearly the heartbeat of God. I could have spent hundreds of pages expounding on the theme of restoration if I wanted to include an exhaustive study of the Scriptures, but any novice can understand the point that restoration was on God's heart from the beginning. His heart for restoration enabled Jesus to endure the cross because of seeing the joy of all of creation brought back to its original intent. We have by no means seen "the restoration of all things," so there must be more on the horizon within the heart and will of God.[439]

Since restoration is on God's heart, He is our best source of finding out what restoration should look like. When it comes to individual restoration, I have used Rev. Jim Bakker as a great example because he ended up where he left off with ministry, favor, impact, and joy. God knows how our Book of Life should read. Jesus is the author and perfecter of faith.[440] Every person has a specific purpose to fulfill, so let us go to the original designer to find out what that purpose is. We cannot give up hope for any person to be restored; the cross of Christ is proof enough for this.

If God could give the original design of the temple and the city structures to David and Solomon, what kind of creativity could come to you for your city? When it came to creating the artifacts to be used with the Tent of Meeting, Bezalel was gifted by the Holy Spirit in the area of creativity to construct everything to fit the design.[441] If God is no respecter of persons, then this ability can be given to anyone today. Can you imagine what would happen if this creativity were given to an entire group of people as they worked together toward restoration?

Surround Yourself with Like-Minded People

I have heard this saying many times: "Bloom where you are planted." But what if the soil is bad? What do you do then? As I pointed out in the case of Joseph, it took a dreamer to restore a dreamer. Within his story, we even see how God worked reconciliation within the restoration of this man and his family. However, the dreams of Joseph were not going to be fulfilled where he was planted with his family.

When it comes to restoration, there must be a group of like-minded people to work with who believe in the same thing. This aspect is clearly demonstrated in the car shop, where all of the members involved in the restoration have the same mindset and agree on what kind of restoration is going to take place. In some cases, they go with the original design. In other cases, the original design gets tweaked to match a new vision. Take my friend Roger, for example, who restored a 1967 Chevelle convertible. Roger stuck with the original maroon metallic paint and the black convertible top but replaced the original 307-cubic-inch engine with a 454-cubic-inch engine and upgraded the transmission and axles to properly handle that kind of power. What would that car have turned out like if even two people did not share the same idea for the car? Thankfully, his wife was on board with him.

When it comes to restoring a person, all of us must be even more careful. Every person is created in the likeness and image of God. Therefore, we must have God's heart for the person, and all must be in agreement of what the final restoration should be. No matter what trespass or character flaw has been exposed, all human limits must be removed. If the restoration idea, for anyone or anything, limits the cross, then it falls short of what God intended.

REFRAME THE VISION

When it comes to vision, two important questions must be asked. The first question is, "Do you have a vision from God that has not yet come to pass?" The second question is, "If you have lost your vision, how do you reframe it so that it can be achieved?" The difficult part of vision is the lack of a tangible physical object that can be observed every day. However, there is a way to make the vision appear so we can perceive it.

In reference to the first question, take a look at Proverbs 29:18: "Where there is no vision, the people are unrestrained, but happy is he who keeps the law."[442] The Hebrew word for "vision" is *khazown*, which means "a revelation, prophecy, vision, or dream."[443] In other words, it is something that comes from God that gives the receiver a glimpse of their potential in the future. The other important word translated *unrestrained* is the Hebrew word *para*, meaning "to neglect, let go, ignore, or let loose."[444] Some translations use the word *perish* because the intent behind neglecting or letting go is not living life actively but falling into passivity, like a trap. Obviously, people will perish unless they get sprung out of the trap.

Thankfully, God gave a way to make the vision tangible. In his time,

Habakkuk could not see how a vision could become reality. But this is what God told him to do: "Record the vision and inscribe it on tablets that the one who reads it may run. For the vision is yet for the appointed time; it hastens toward the goal and it will not fail. Though it tarries wait for it; for it will certainly come, it will not delay."[445] Endurance is necessary.

The only way to change our thoughts is through the lips and through the fingertips. We must write something down, because it actually engages different parts of our brain when we do this. Then we must speak out what we have written. If we think that we cannot do something, then we will not do it. We can interrupt that thought with words. Even God spoke creation into existence. We are created in His image and likeness. We engage a different level of creativity when we produce something through both writing and speaking.

GUARD AND GARNER YOUR HEART

In the restoration process, challenges will come. When these challenges come, they usually manifest when we are at our lowest. This is why it is so important to have the vision framed in writing so that it cannot be stolen or altered. We were also forewarned by the sage who wrote this proverb: "Watch over your heart with all diligence, for from it flows the springs of life."[446] It can be difficult to overcome an enemy. It can be even harder to overcome ourselves. The author made this metaphor like watchmen on the wall who had to be alert at all times and could not doze off on their shift. One tactic of the enemy in that era involved removing the water supply. If the well was poisoned, all life would be choked out.

The best way to guard our hearts is with the peace of God. The apostle Paul wrote, "And the God of peace shall soon crush Satan under your feet."[447] Notice that he did not say "the God of love" or "the God of power," even though those are also who He is. *Peace*, from the Hebrew word *shalom*, is what we have again with the heart of "nothing missing, nothing broken." This kind of peace also applies to every facet of your life, including finances, relationships, family, social standing, physical health, mental health, and spiritual health. Paul also wrote, "And the peace of God, which transcends all comprehension, shall guard your hearts and minds in Christ Jesus."[448] We do not have to understand it in order to keep it. I have had peace—in the midst of storms or under fire—that was unexplainable. When that peace is obtained, guard it like a hidden treasure.

Redefine the Future

The future is created today. If we want to change what the future will look like, we must be intentional with every thought, word, and deed in this day. On October 31, 1517, Martin Luther may not have fully intended to spark a reformation by nailing his Ninety-Five Theses on the door of his church in Wittenberg, Germany, but his future changed after that day, along with all of Europe and Christendom. The future has been recorded as Reformation Day.

Following an ugly divorce, one minister, whom I'll call "Scott," lost his church along with his ordination from the movement that he had been a part of for over a decade. The circumstances, along with this particular movement, decided what his future would be by the actions they took in the present. Scott could have kept the script that these other agencies developed for his life. But he had an opportunity to rewrite his own ending. Scott knew, within his own heart, that God's calling and his gifting were not going to change, regardless of the circumstances.[449]

Some people knew Scott's divorce was not due to pornography, adultery, or any abuse but from his wife's affair with another man. These Paraclete People in his life took the time to speak into Scott's life and encourage him to pursue his purpose. The Paraclete People also shared a new vision that Scott had received, thus confirming that God had a plan that he needed to grab. Scott captured these new ideas and wrote them out. He found a safe place to write out his ideas and put them into practice within a new community and new church that he is now leading.

Turning Ideas into Action

I have shared my ideas, and my hope is that God has inspired ideas inside of you of how to obtain restoration in your own life. Habakkuk stated that a person would need to run with the vision. This speaks of action and movement. Like Scott, perhaps God has placed a vision on your heart to help ignite the Restoration Reformation. We have had all kinds of shows in relation to restoring cars, houses, and antiques, but what about a culture shift toward spiritual restoration of the lost, wounded, and fallen? What would happen if churches started having restoration conferences? What if different Christian movements established centers of restoration? Furthermore, what if different Christian movements united to have centers of restoration throughout different regions of our own nation and then around the world?

With the creativity of God, there is not a glass ceiling to hold anyone back. If anyone can grab a pen and paper, then anyone can take their creative ideas and formulate a plan that is tailored to a specific situation. We do not want to be like the head of the US Patent Office in 1902, thinking that "everything that could possibly be invented has already been invented."[450] We have only scratched the surface that has revealed an infinite number of possibilities that are waiting to be discovered.

We cannot steer a parked car, so even if we start in reverse, at least we can be moving. Some people may be overly cautious, making sure the route is completely safe before leaving, but then, how much delay is involved? As a man, I conquer vacations and do my best to get to the destination as quickly as possible. The best part of movement is that the direction can be changed or the course can be corrected, and we will eventually reach the goal of our destination. If we were to park in the middle of a desert or stop in the middle of a blizzard, either scenario leaves little chance of survival. In order to start a movement, somebody must get moving. So, are you with me to put your ideas and mine into action?

POINTS TO PONDER

1. How many times has someone tried to keep you in a box that they have built for you and your life?
2. What are we willing to sacrifice to see the restoration come to pass?
3. Can you imagine if this creativity was given to an entire group of people as they worked together toward restoration?
4. Do you have a vision from God that has not yet come to pass?
5. If you have lost your vision, how will you reframe it so that it can be achieved?
6. We have had all kinds of shows in relation to restoring cars, houses, and antiques, but what about a culture shift toward spiritual restoration of the lost, wounded, and fallen?
7. Are you with me to put your ideas and mine into action?

RESOURCES

Assisting Agencies, Ministries, and People

Cleansing Stream Ministries at https://www.cleansingstream.org. They have a reputation for helping people with a proven track record going back decades.

Discovery! Austin is a safe venue where you can go and be genuine about your life and receive healing, comfort, and purpose. Learn more at http://www.discovery-austin.org.

Doug Addison is a life coach, dream interpreter, and comedian! Having overcome so much, he is unique in assisting others at http://dougaddison.com.

Lance Learning Group, Inc. Dr. Lance Wallnau has a gift for helping people overcome their past hurts and failures and encourages them to launch out into their life purpose on the Seven Mountains of Culture, www.lancelearning.com.

Marked Men for Christ and Women Walking with Christ provides a safe space with a group of like-minded people who want to be genuine and free. https://www.markedmenforchrist.org/Default.aspx.

MorningStar Ministries has a reputation for getting people to know God's plan, get equipped for God's purposes, and be fully restored in order to demonstrate what God is capable of accomplishing—the impossible. They can be explored at www.morningstarministries.org.

Pure Desire Ministries International can be reached at http://www. puredesire.org. Many people get caught up in sexual issues due to past grief, loss, and trauma. Dr. Ted Roberts speaks with authority and experience of how to break free of these addictions.

Restoring the Foundations (RTF), International at https://www. restoringthefoundations.org. They have a network of counselors across the United States and can work with individuals or couples.

The Jim Bakker Show has proven to be a voice for our times concerning restoration and how Christians must mobilize to see the kingdom of God extended. The show can be reached at https://jimbakkershow.com/.

The truth has power in any form. Ultimately, from my experience, the truth is a person named Jesus, and He can assist you getting completely free and restored (see John 8:32–36; 14:6).

Books

Addison, Doug. *Understand Your Dreams Now: Spiritual Dream Interpretation* (Santa Maria, CA: InLight Connection, 2013).

Andrews, Andy. *Storms of Perfection* (Nashville, TN: Lightning Crown Publishers, 1991).

Augustine of Hippo. *The City of God*, translated by Marcus Dods (Peabody, MA: Hendrickson Publishers, Inc., 2010).

The Bible! This one book has all things pertaining to life and godliness. Pick a translation and pick a language—the best-selling book of all time!

Bruce-Hamburger, Shauna. *Beyond Adversity into Freedom* (Sevierville, TN: Insight Publishing Co., 2010). Find more at www.divinepotential.com.

Frankl, Viktor. *Man's Search for Meaning* (Boston, Massachusetts: Beacon Press, 1959).

Enlow, Johnny. *The Seven Mountain Mantle: Receiving the Joseph Anointing to Reform Nations* (Lake Mary, FL: Creation House, 2009).

Hamon, Jane. *Dreams and Visions: Understanding and Interpreting God's Messages to You* (Minneapolis, MN: Chosen, 2016).

Hillman, Os. Change agent: *Engaging Your Passion to Be the One Who Makes a Difference* (Charisma House, 2011).

Jackson, John Paul. *Moments with God Dream Journal* (North Sutton, NH: Streams Publications, 2002).

Joyner, Rick. *I See a New America* (Ft. Mill, SC: Quest Ventures, 2011).

Rodriguez, Samuel. *You Are Next: Destroy What Has Paralyzed You, and Never Miss Your Moment Again* (Lake Mary, FL: Charisma House, 2019).

Seahorn, Janet J. and E. Anthony. *Tears of a Warrior: A Family's Story of Combat and Living with PTSD* (Ft. Collins, CO: Team Pursuits, 2008). Find more at www.teampursuits.com.

Sheets, Dutch, *Tell Your Heart to Beat Again* (Ventura, CA: Gospel Light Publications, 2002). Find more at www.dutchsheets.org.

Notes

1   John Mellencamp, "Jack and Diane," off the *American Fool* Album (Riva Records, 1982).

2   1 Corinthians 13:8. "THE THOMPSON CHAIN-REFERENCE® BIBLE," (Indianapolis, IN: B.B. KIRKBRIDE BIBLE COMPANY, INC., 1993. "Scripture taken from the NEW AMERICAN STANDARD BIBLE, ©1960, 1962, 1963, 1968, 1971, 1972, 1973, 1975, 1977, by The Lockman Foundation.

3   Acts 3:19–21.

4   1 Corinthians 14:33.

5   Matthew 5:44.

6   John 10:10.

7   John 10:10.

8   Michael Howard and Peter Paret, ed., *Carl Von Clausewitz: On War* (Princeton, NJ: Princeton University Press, 1989), p. 65.

9   Merriam-Webster, Incorporated, "Restoration Definition," *www.merriam-webster.com*, accessed August 10, 2019, https://www.merriam-webster.com/dictionary/restoration.

10   Blue Letter Bible Institute, "Definition of Peace, Strong's Reference H7965, *www.blueletterbibile.org*, accessed August 10, 2019, https://www.blueletterbible.org/lang/lexicon/lexicon.cfm?Strongs=H7965&t=NASB.

11   Sophia Smith, "The Japanese Art of Recognizing Beauty in Broken Things," *www.makezine.com*, August 17, 2015, https://makezine.com/2015/08/17/kintsugi-japanese-art-recognizing-beauty-broken-things/.

12   Smith, "The Japanese Art of Recognizing Beauty in Broken Things."

13   Proverbs 14:10.

14   Liz Leafloor, "Symbolism of the Mythical Phoenix Bird: Renewal, Rebirth, and Destruction," www.ancient-origins.net, 24 March 2019, https://www.ancient-origins.net/myths-legends/ancient-symbolism-magical-phoenix-002020.

15   Acts 3:20–21.

16   Michael Graham, "The Inerrancy of Scripture: A Doctrine under Fire," *Diligence: Journal of the Liberty University Online Religion Capstone in Research and Scholarship*

1, article 13 (September 2016): 1–16, https://digitalcommons.liberty.edu/cgi/viewcontent.cgi?article=1020&context=djrc.

17 The Net Study Bible, "The Biblical Law of First Mention," *www.netbiblestudy.com*, accessed November 18, 2018, http://netbiblestudy.com/00_cartimages/thelawoffirstmention.pdf.

18 Genesis 1:1.

19 Blue Letter Bible Institute, "Definition of Moving," Strong's Reference H7363, *www.blueletterbible.org*, accessed August 10, 2019, https://www.blueletterbible.org/lang/lexicon/lexicon.cfm?Strongs=H7363&t=NASB.

20 Genesis 1:12–13.

21 Blue Letter Bible Institute, "Definition of Seed," Strong's Reference H2233, *www.blueletterbible.org*, accessed 10 August 2019, https://www.blueletterbible.org/lang/lexicon/lexicon.cfm?Strongs=H2233&t=NASB.

22 1 Corinthians 15:4.

23 Genesis 2:9.

24 Genesis 2:16–17.

25 Genesis 3:17–18.

26 Genesis 3:21.

27 Genesis 3:15.

28 Luke 1:26–38; 42.

29 Genesis 8:22.

30 See Genesis 9:8–15.

31 Genesis 12:2–3.

32 See Genesis 14.

33 Genesis 14:19–20.

34 Hebrews 7:2.

35 Blue Letter Bible Institute, "Definition of Righteousness," Strong's Reference H6664, *www.blueletterbible.org*, accessed 17 August 2019, https://www.blueletterbible.org/lang/lexicon/lexicon.cfm?strongs=H6664&t=NASB.

36 Blue Letter Bible Institute, "Definition of Peace," Strong's Reference H6664, *www.blueletterbible.org*, accessed 17 August 2019, https://www.blueletterbible.org/lang/lexicon/lexicon.cfm?strongs=H8003&t=NASB.

37 Genesis 49:10.

38 1 Samuel 13:13–14.

39 Genesis 49:10.

40 Psalm 23:1.

41 Psalm 23:3.

42 Psalm 51:10–12.

43 Isaiah 5:20.

44 Isaiah 9:1–2;6–7.

45 Isaiah 11:6–9.

46   Isaiah 60:1–3.

47   Matthew 1:23.

48   Luke 4:18–19.

49   John 1:29.

50   Leviticus 17:11.

51   Isaiah 53:3–5.

52   Deuteronomy 21:22–23.

53   Deuteronomy 21:22–23.

54   Genesis 3:15.

55   1 Corinthians 15:45.

56   John 13:23–25.

57   John 20:15, italics mine.

58   Genesis 2:15.

59   John 3:16.

60   Blue Letter Bible Institute, "Definition of World," Strong's Reference G2889, *www.blueletterbible.org*, accessed 17 August 2019, https://www.blueletterbible. org/lang/lexicon/lexicon.cfm?Strongs=G2889&t=NASB.

61   John 19:2.

62   Matthew 27:35.

63   Romans 8:19–22.

64   2 Peter 3:9.

65   Revelation 5:9.

66   Revelation 5:9.

67   Acts 3:21.

68   Mathew 10:41a, my emphasis on gender inclusion.

69   Acts 3:21.

70   2 Kings 4:8.

71   2 Kings 4:8.

72   2 Kings 4:9.

73   2 Kings 4:10.

74   2 Kings 4:14.

75   2 Kings 4:14.

76   2 Kings 4:14–15.

77   2 Kings 4:16.

78   2 Kings 4:18.

79   2 Kings 4:19.

80   2 Kings 4:20.

81   2 Kings 4:21–24.

82   2 Kings 4:25.

83   2 Kings 4:25–27.

84   2 Kings 4:26, emphasis mine.

85 2 Kings 4:29–31.

86 2 Kings 4:32–35.

87 2 Kings 4:37.

88 2 Kings 8:1.

89 Proverbs 16:7.

90 2 Kings 8:4–5.

91 2 Kings 8:5.

92 2 Kings 8:6.

93 2 Kings 8:6.

94 2 Kings 8:6.

95 Numbers 23:19, Malachi 3:6, respectively.

96 Acts 10:34.

97 Acts 3:19–21.

98 Hebrews 6:12.

99 Romans 12:15.

100 Wade A. Jensen, *The Pathological Grieving of America: Overcoming Grief on a Personal, Corporate and National Scale* (Seattle, WA: Kindle Direct Publishing, 2014).

101 1 Samuel 29:6.

102 Blue Letter Bible Institute, "Definition of Ziklag," Strong's Reference H6860, *www.blueletterbibile.org*, accessed 21 September 2019, https://www.blueletterbible.org/lang/lexicon/lexicon.cfm?Strongs=H6860&t=NASB.

103 1 Samuel 27:7.

104 1 Samuel 30:1–3.

105 1 Samuel 30:3–4.

106 1 Samuel 30:6.

107 1 Samuel 30:6.

108 Blue Letter Bible Institute, "Definition of Abiathar," Strong's Reference H54, *www.blueletterbibile.org*, accessed 21 September 2019, https://www.blueletterbible.org/lang/lexicon/lexicon.cfm?Strongs=H54&t=NASB.

109 1 Samuel 30:7.

110 1 Samuel 30:8.

111 1 Samuel 30:9–10.

112 1 Samuel 30:11–14.

113 1 Samuel 30:15.

114 1 Samuel 30:16–17.

115 1 Samuel 30:18–19.

116 1 Samuel 30:20.

117 1 Samuel 30:22.

118 1 Samuel 30:23–24.

119 See 1 Samuel 24:1–22; 1 Samuel 26:1–25.

120 1 Samuel 26:9.

121 2 Samuel 11:1.

122 2 Samuel 11:2.

123 2 Samuel 11:3.

124 2 Samuel 11:5.

125 2 Samuel 11:11.

126 2 Samuel 11:15.

127 2 Samuel 23:39.

128 2 Samuel 12:5–6.

129 2 Samuel 12:7.

130 2 Samuel 12:7–12.

131 2 Samuel 12:13.

132 1 Samuel 16:7.

133 2 Samuel 12:20.

134 Psalm 51:1–19.

135 2 Samuel 12:25.

136 2 Samuel 12:30.

137 2 Samuel 13:32–33.

138 2 Samuel 16:22; 2 Samuel 20:3.

139 *The Holy Bible*, English Standard Version, 2 Corinthians 13:11a (Wheaton, IL: Crossway Books and Bibles, a Publishing Ministry of Good News Publishers, 2001, 2007, 2011, 2016).

140 Psalm 23:3.

141 Gal 6:1–2.

142 Jennifer Rosenberg, "The Jonestown Massacre," *www.thoughtco.com*, accessed 25 May 2019, https://www.thoughtco.com/the-jonestown-massacre-1779385.

143 1 Peter 4:17.

144 Ephesians 2:2.

145 Andrew G. Coyle, "Prison: Emergence of the Penitentiary," *www.britannica.com*, accessed 23 April 2019, https://www.britannica.com/topic/prison.

146 Psalm 14:1–3; Psalm 53:1–3.

147 Harry Elmer Barnes, "Historial Origin of the Prison System in America," 12 *J. Am. Inst. Crim. L. & Criminology 35* (May 1921 to February 1922), https://scholarlycommons.law.northwestern.edu/cgi/viewcontent.cgi?article=1772&context=jclc, 37.

148 Genesis 39:6–20.

149 Genesis 39:6–20.

150 Genesis 39:21

151 Bakker, *I Was Wrong*, p. 198.

152 Bakker, *I Was Wrong*, p. 199.

153 Bakker, *I Was Wrong*, p. 199.

154 Genesis 41:1–16.

155 Bakker, *I Was Wrong*, p. 290.

156 Bakker, *I Was Wrong*, p. 321.

157 Malachi 4:2.

158 Malachi 4:2.

159 Reverence Definition, *www.merriam-webster.com*, accessed 18 April 2019, https://www.merriam-webster.com/dictionary/reverence.

160 Malachi 4:2.

161 Blue Letter Bible Institute, "Definition of Righteousness," Strong's Reference H6666, *www.blueletterbible.org*, accessed 10 August 2019, https://www.blueletterbible.org/lang/lexicon/lexicon.cfm?Strongs=H6666&t=NASB.

162 Blue Letter Bible Institute, "Definition of Peace," Strong's Reference H7965, *www.blueletterbible.org*, accessed 10 August 2019, https://www.blueletterbible.org/lang/lexicon/lexicon.cfm?Strongs=H7965&t=NASB.

163 Bakker, *I Was Wrong*, p. 134.

164 Bakker, *I Was Wrong*, p. 134.

165 165 Bakker, *I Was Wrong*, p. 282–283.

166 Bakker, *I Was Wrong*, p. 283.

167 Bakker, *I Was Wrong*, Title Page.

168 Proverbs 18:22.

169 Merriam-Webster, "The Definition of Paradox," *www.merriam-webster.com*, accessed 22 June 2019, https://www.merriam-webster.com/dictionary/paradox.

170 Galatians 6:1.

171 Genesis 37:1–11.

172 Genesis 37:2.

173 Genesis 37:3.

174 Genesis 37:12–13.

175 Genesis 37:20–22.

176 Genesis 37:22, emphasis mine.

177 Genesis 37:28.

178 Genesis 37:31.

179 Genesis 37:33.

180 Genesis 37:36.

181 Genesis 37:36.

182 Genesis 39:3.

183 Genesis 39:5.

184 Genesis 39:6–9.

185 Genesis 39:12.

186 Genesis 39:14–17.

187 Genesis 39:21.

188 Genesis 39:22–23.

189 Genesis 40:6.

190 Genesis 40:8.

191 Genesis 40:13.

192 Genesis 40:16–17.

193 Genesis 40:18–22.

194 Genesis 41:1–13.

195 Genesis 41:24.

196 Genesis 41:14–24.

197 Genesis 41:16.

198 Genesis 41:25, 28.

199 Genesis 41:32.

200 2 Corinthians 13:11, my emphasis on the actual Greek word translated as "matter."

201 Genesis 41:33–37.

202 Genesis 41:39–42.

203 Acts 13:1–5.

204 Acts 13:5.

205 Acts 13:13.

206 Galatians 6:1.

207 Acts 15:37.

208 Acts 15:38–39.

209 Acts 11:22–26.

210 John 16:8–11.

211 Romans 11:29.

212 Galatians 5:19–23.

213 Proverbs 11:14.

214 John 14:26.

215 Proverbs 4:23.

216 Acts 3:18–21.

217 Blue Letter Bible Institute, "Definition of Times," Strong's Reference G2540, *www.blueletterbible.org*, accessed 22 October 2019, https://www.blueletterbible.org/lang/lexicon/lexicon.cfm?Strongs=G2540&t=NASB.

218 Blue Letter Bible Institute, "Definition of Refreshing," Strong's Reference G403, *www.blueletterbible.org*, accessed 22 October 2019, https://www.blueletterbible.org/lang/lexicon/lexicon.cfm?ot=NASB&strongs=G403&t=NASB#lexSearch.

219 Blue Letter Bible Institute, "Definition of Period in Acts 3:21," Strong's Reference G5550, *www.blueletterbible.org*, accessed 22 October 2019, https://www.blueletterbible.org/lang/lexicon/lexicon.cfm?Strongs=G5550&t=NASB.

220 Proverbs 13:12.

221 Merriam-Webster, "The Definition of Paradox," www.*merriam-webster.com*, accessed 22 June 2019, https://www.merriam-webster.com/dictionary/paradox.

222 Exodus 3:6.

223 2 Peter 3:8.
224 Psalm 89:14.
225 Revelation 19:2.
226 Job 42:12–16.
227 Genesis 15:13.
228 Genesis 41:1–37.
229 Genesis 41:8.
230 Genesis 41:41.
231 Genesis 50:15–18.
232 Exodus 1:8.
233 Exodus 2:23–24.
234 Exodus 2:14.
235 Exodus 12:35–36.
236 Hebrews 4:19.
237 Joshua 14:6–15.
238 Joshua 14:10–11.
239 Genesis 3:1–19.
240 Genesis 3:21.
241 Genesis 3:22–24.
242 2 Corinthians 5:17.
243 John 16:8–11.
244 Jeremiah 52:12–27.
245 2 Chronicles 36:21.
246 Jeremiah 27:22.
247 Daniel 1:3–5.
248 Daniel 9:20–27.
249 Isaiah 45:1–7.
250 Genesis 33:18–19.
251 John 4:5–6.
252 Matthew 1:17.
253 Numerology Center, "Biblical Numerology – Number 14," *www.numerology. center,* accessed 12 August 2020, http://numerology.center/biblical_numbers_ number_14.php.
254 John 4:1–26.
255 Acts 3:21
256 John 5:19.
257 Deuteronomy 19:15.
258 Exodus 34:6–7.
259 Proverbs 3:9.
260 Joshua 6:26.
261 1 Kings 16:34.

262 Blue Letter Bible Institute, "Definition of Hiel," Strong's Reference H2419, *www.blueletterbible.org*, accessed 22 October 2019, https://www.blueletterbible.org/lexicon/h2419/nkjv/wlc/0-1/.

263 Genesis 28:17–19.

264 2 Kings 2:19.

265 2 Kings 2:21.

266 Mark 10:46–52.

267 Luke 19:1–10.

268 Exodus 3:6.

269 Acts 10:34.

270 Hebrews 6:12.

271 Habakkuk 2:2.

272 Proverbs 29:18.

273 Ezra 3:12–13.

274 Habakkuk 2:3.

275 James M. Kouzes & Barry Z. Posner, *The Leadership Challenge, Sixth ed.: How to Make Extraordinary Things Happen in Organizations* (Hoboken, NJ: John Wiley & Sons, Inc., 2017), pp. 95–106.

276 Stephen Covey, The 7 Habits of Highly Effective People: Powerful Lessons in Personal Change. (New York, NY: Simon and Schuster, 2004) pp. 52–100.

277 Hank Coleman, "The SMART Way to Accomplishing Your Goals," *www.themilit arywallet.com*, 6 May 2019, https://themilitarywallet.com/create-smart-goals/.

278 Hank Coleman, "The SMART Way to Accomplishing Your Goals," *www.themilitarywallet.com*, 6 May 2019, https://themilitarywallet.com/create-smart-goals/.

279 Genesis 1:26–28.

280 Exodus 34:1.

281 Habakkuk 2:3.

282 Luke 14:28.

283 1 Corinthians 12:12–27.

284 Habakkuk 2:2.

285 John P. Kotter, *John P. Kotter on what Leaders Really Do* (Cambridge, MA: Harvard Business School Press, 1999), p. 54.

286 2 Corinthians 3:18.

287 Jenni Marsh, "Tadao Ando: The Japanese Boxer Turned Pritzker Prize Winner Who Buried the Buddha," www.*cnn.com*, 5 November 2017, https://edition.cnn.com/style/article/tadao-ando-exhibition/index.html.

288 Jenni Marsh, "Tadao Ando: The Japanese Boxer Turned Pritzker Prize Winner Who Buried the Buddha," www.*cnn.com*, 5 November 2017, https://edition.cnn.com/style/article/tadao-ando-exhibition/index.html.

289 Proverbs 4:18.

290 Isaiah 58:12.

291 Genesis 4:17.

292 Blue Letter Bible Institute, "Definition of City," Strong's Reference H5892, *www.blueletterbible.org,* accessed 22 July 2020, https://www.blueletterbible.org/lang/lexicon/lexicon.cfm?Strongs=H5892&t=NKJV.

293 Blue Letter Bible Institute, "Definition of Enoch," Strong's Reference H2585, *www.blueletterbible.org,* accessed 22 July 2020, https://www.blueletterbible.org/lang/lexicon/lexicon.cfm?Strongs=H2585&t=NKJV.

294 Genesis 17:8.

295 Daniel 9:2.

296 Dr. Gary Greig, "The Biblical Foundations of Identificational Repentance as One Prayer Pattern Useful to Advance God's Kingdom and Evangelism," www.cwgministries.org, accessed 4 August 2020, https://www.cwgministries.org/books/Biblical-Foundation-for-Identificational-Repentance.pdf.

297 Isaiah 58:6–7.

298 Isaiah 58:12.

299 Isaiah 58:14.

300 Psalm 127:1.

301 The Editors of Encyclopaedia Britannica, "The Hasmonean Dynasty," www.britannica.com, accessed 5 August 2020, https://www.britannica.com/topic/Hasmonean-dynasty.

302 Committee for Middle East Reporting in America (CAMERA), "1967: Reunification of Jerusalem," www.*sixdaywar.org,* accessed 5 August 2020, http://www.sixdaywar.org/content/ReunificationJerusalem.asp.

303 Psalm 122:6.

304 Michael Miller, "The Real Grizzly Man: The Amazing True Story Behind Leonardo DiCaprio's Character in *The Revenant,*" www.*people.com,* 6 January 2016, https://people.com/movies/leonardo-dicaprio-s-revenant-character-the-true-story-of-hugh-glass/.

305 Lauren Donovan, "Lemmon, SD, site for movie premier of 'The Revenant,'" www.*inforum.com,* 26 December 2015, https://www.inforum.com/entertainment/3910664-lemmon-sd-site-movie-premiere-revenant.

306 Matthew 5:44.

307 Translated by Liam Walsh, "Rebuilding Hiroshima-Akio Nishikiori: Atomic Bombing Survivor, Architect," *www.antnewshiroshima-nagasaki.net,* 25 May 2019 , http://antnews.hiroshima-nagasaki.net/rebuilding-hiroshima-akio-nishikiori-atomic-bombing-survivor-architect/.

308 Translated by Liam Walsh, "Rebuilding Hiroshima-Akio Nishikiori: Atomic Bombing Survivor, Architect," *www.antnewshiroshima-nagasaki.net,* 25 May 2019, http://antnews.hiroshima-nagasaki.net/rebuilding-hiroshima-akio-nishikiori-atomic-bombing-survivor-architect/.

309 Translated by Liam Walsh, "Rebuilding Hiroshima-Akio Nishikiori: Atomic Bombing Survivor, Architect," *www.antnewshiroshima-nagasaki.net*, 25 May 2019 , http://antnews.hiroshima-nagasaki.net/rebuilding-hiroshima-akio-nishikiori-atomic-bombing-survivor-architect/.

310 1 Peter 4:8.

311 "Berlin at the end of the War, 1945," *www.rarehistoricalphotos.com,* accessed 6 August 2020, https://rarehistoricalphotos.com/berlin-end-war-1945/.

312 "Berlin at the end of the War, 1945," *www.rarehistoricalphotos.com,* accessed 6 August 2020, https://rarehistoricalphotos.com/berlin-end-war-1945/.

313 CRAM, "John Fitzgerald Kennedy's Speech: Ich Bin Ein Berliner," www.*cram. com*, accessed 6 August 2020, https://www.cram.com/essay/John-Fitzgerald-Kennedys-Speech-Ich-Bin-Ein/FKN4JUAY7BQW.

314 Revelation 21:2.

315 Blue Letter Bible Institute, "Definition of New," Strong's Reference G2537, *www.blueletterbible.org*, accessed 24 July 2020, https://www.blueletterbible.org/lang/lexicon/lexicon.cfm?Strongs=G2537&t=NKJV.

316 Josh Margolin, "1 World Trade Center Highlights Rebirth, Renewal Following 9/11 Attacks," *www.abcnews.go.com*, 3 November 2014, https://abcnews.go.com/US/world-trade-center-opening-highlights-rebirth-renewal-911/story?id=26649497.

317 Isaiah 55:5a.

318 Psalm 2:8.

319 Genesis 1:26–28.

320 Genesis 12:2.

321 Blue Letter Bible Institute, "Definition of Nation," Strong's Reference H1471, *www.blueletterbible.org,* accessed 23 August 2020, https://www.blueletterbible.org/lang/lexicon/lexicon.cfm?Strongs=H1471&t=NASB.

322 Blue Letter Bible Institute, "LXX of Genesis 12:2," *www.blueletterbible.org,* accessed 23 August 2020,https://www.blueletterbible.org/nasb/gen/12/2/p0/t_conc_12002.

323 Blue Letter Bible Institute, "Definition of Country," Strong's Reference H2022, *www.blueletterbible.org,* accessed 23 August 2020, https://www.blueletterbible.org/lang/lexicon/lexicon.cfm?Strongs=H2022&t=NASB.

324 Blue Letter Bible Institute, "Definition of Country," Strong's Reference H776, *www.blueletterbible.org,* accessed 23 August 2020, https://www.blueletterbible.org/lang/lexicon/lexicon.cfm?Strongs=H776&t=NASB.

325 Blue Letter Bible Institute, "Definition of Kingdom," Strong's Reference H4467, *www.blueletterbible.org,* accessed 23 August 2020, https://www.blueletterbible.org/lang/lexicon/lexicon.cfm?Strongs=H4467&t=NASB.

326 Revelation 7:9.

327 Revelation 11:15.

328 D ic tionary.com, LLC, "The Definition of Apathy," www.*dictionary.com*, accessed 25 August 2020, https://www.dictionary.com/browse/apathy.

329 W. O'Daniel, "Victorian London, - Crime - Prostitution - Numbers of Prostitutes," www.*victorianlondon.org, Ins and Outs of London*, 1859, accessed 8 December 2020, https://www.victorianlondon.org/crime/numbersofprostitutes.htm.

330 Andrea Curry, "Abolitionist William Wilberforce and the British Slave Trade," *www.britishheritage.com,* 8 October 2020, accessed 8 December 2020, https://britishheritage.com/history/the-abolition-of-the-slave-trade.

331 Genesis 6:11.

332 Hebrews 4:16.

333 Psalm 89:14.

334 James 5:17–18.

335 1 Peter 4:17.

336 2 Chronicles 7:13–14.

337 Blue Letter Bible Institute, "Definition of Heal," Strong's Reference H7495, *www.blueletterbible.org,* accessed 25 August 2020, https://www.blueletterbible.org/lang/lexicon/lexicon.cfm?Strongs=H7495&t=NASB.

338 James 4:6.

339 2 Chronicles 7:14.

340 Jeremiah 5:1; Ezekiel 22:30.

341 Jonah 3:5–10.

342 2 Samuel 24:10, Exodus 30:12.

343 2 Samuel 6:11.

344 2 Chronicles 5:13–14.

345 Leviticus 26:14-39.

346 Leviticus 26:40-46.

347 Isaiah 60:1–5.

348 Acts 2:4.

349 Jeremiah 1:10.

350 Matthew 28:19.

351 Ezekiel 22:30.

352 Judges 7:7.

353 Dutch Sheets, "We Need to Love America," *www.giveHim15.com*, 13 August, 2020, http://givehim15.com/blog/page/2/.

354 Abram Van Engen, "How America Became a City upon a Hill: The Rise and Fall of Perry Miller," *Humanities, Winter 2020, Vol. 41, No. 1,* https://www.neh.gov/article/how-america-became-city-upon-hill.

355 H is tory.com Editors, "Thomas Paine Publishes "The American Crisis,"" A & E Television Networks, *www.history.com*, accessed16 December 2019, accessed 25 August 2020, https://www.history.com/this-day-in-history/thomas-paine-publishes-american-crisis.

356 John 3:16.

357 Daniel Block, "Is Trump Our Cyrus? The Old Testament Case for Yes and No," *www.christianitytoday.com*, 29 October 2018, https://www.christianitytoday.com/ct/2018/october-web-only/donald-trump-cyrus-prophecy-old-testament.html.

358 Leviticus 25:8-17.

359 Rare Historical Photos, "German Soldiers React to Footage of Concentration Camps," *www.rarehistoricalphotos.com,* accessed 8 December 2020, https://rarehistoricalphotos.com/german-soldiers-forced-watch-footage-concentration-camps-1945/.

360 Romans 5:20.

361 Deming Collaboration and Rafael Aguayo, "Who Was W. Edwards Deming?" ✓ *www.demingcollaboration.com*, 2010, accessed 8 December 2020, https://demingcollaboration.com/w-edwards-deming/who-was-w-edwards-deming/.

362 Galatians 6:9.

363 Genesis 8:22.

364 Sebastien Roblin, "Forget the Coronavirus: The Flu Pandemic of 1918 Killed More People in One Year than all of World War I," *www.news.yahoo.com,* 15 February 2020, accessed 8 December 2020, https://news.yahoo.com/forget-coronavirus-flu-pandemic-1918-140000412.html.

365 John 16:33.

366 Isaiah 59:19, my punctuation.

367 Revelation 3:8.

368 Henry Blackaby & Claude King, *Experiencing God: Knowing and Doing the Will of God,* (Nashville, TN: Lifeway Press, 1990), p. 15.

369 Acts 17:26.

370 Matthew 25:32.

371 Matthew 19:26.

372 Matthew 28:19–20, translation according to Greek text and emphasis, mine.

373 Psalm 2:8.

374 Acts 3:21.

375 Malachi 4:5–6.

376 Os Hillman, *Change Agent: Engaging Your Passion to Be the One Who Makes a Difference* (Lake Mary, FL: Charisma House, 2011), pp. 101–210.

377 Joshua 14:12.

378 Amos 9:11–12.

379 The Merriam-Webster Dictionary, "Definition of Paradox," *www.merriam-webster.com*, accessed 11 June 2019, https://www.merriam-webster.com/dictionary/paradox.

380 1 Samuel 13:1–13; 15:1–22.

381 2 Samuel 12:13.

382 2 Samuel 12: 13–20.

383 Romans 6:23.

384 Acts 15:36–41.

385 Acts 3:19.

386 Matthew 22:37–40.

387 John Arnott, "The Toronto Blessing: What Is It?" *www.johnandcarol.org*, 31 December 1999, accessed 8 December 2020, http://www.johnandcarol.org/updates/the-toronto-blessing-what-is-it.

388 Ephesians 5:18.

389 2 Timothy 1:6.

390 2 Corinthians 13:11.

391 Blue Letter Bible Institute, "Definition of Peace," Strong's Reference H6664, *www.blueletterbible.org,* accessed 17 August 2019, https://www.blueletterbible.org/lang/lexicon/lexicon.cfm?strongs=H8003&t=NASB.

392 Galatians 6:1.

393 Proverbs 24:16.

394 Matthew 18:22.

395 Dictionary.com, LLC, "Definition of Principle," *www.dictionary.com*, Accessed 5 February 2020, https://www.dictionary.com/browse/principle.

396 Dictionary.com, LLC, "Definition of Process," *www.dictionary.com*, Accessed 5 February 2020, https://www.dictionary.com/browse/process?s=t.

397 James 5:16.

398 Blue Letter Bible, "The meaning of Iaomai," *www.blueletterbible.org*, Accessed 6 February 2020, https://www.blueletterbible.org/lang/lexicon/lexicon.cfm?Strongs=G2390&t=NASB.

399 Romans 11:29.

400 Galatians 5:22–23.

401 Galatians 6:1.

402 Blue Letter Bible, "The meaning of Israel," *www.blueletterbible.org*, Accessed 7 February 2020, https://www.www.blueletterbible.org/lang/lexicon/lexicon.cfm?Strongs=H3478&t=NASB.

403 Blue Letter Bible, "The meaning of Jabez," *www.blueletterbible.org*, Accessed 7 February 2020, https://www.blueletterbible.org/lang/lexicon/lexicon.cfm?Strongs=H3258&t=NASB.

404 1 Chronicles 4:9.

405 1 Chronicles 4:10.

406 W. Dean Dyk, "Performance Quote," 10 October 2005, Swedish Medical Center, Englewood, CO.

407 Matthew 13:23.

408 Luke 12:48.

409 Galatians 6:1.

410 John 14:16.

411 Acts 6:5.

412 Galatians 6:1.

413 Blue Letter Bible, "The meaning of Spiritual," *www.blueletterbible.org*, Accessed May 2020, https://www.blueletterbible.org/lang/lexicon/inflections.cfm?strongs=G4151&t=KJV&ot=TR&word=%CF%80%CE%BD%CE%B5%E1%BD%BB%CE%BC%CE%B1%CF%84%CE%B9.

414 Acts 6:5.

415 Galatians 6:1.

416 Blue Letter Bible, "The meaning of Gentleness," *www.blueletterbible.org*, Accessed 25 May 2020, https://www.blueletterbible.org/lang/lexicon/lexicon.cfm?Strongs=G4236&t=KJV.

417 1 Timothy 3:6.

418 Galatians 6:1–10.

419 1 Timothy 5:18.

420 Genesis 28:12.

421 Genesis 28:17.

422 Numbers 35:9–34.

423 Galatians 6:1.

424 2 Samuel 2:1–7.

425 1 Corinthians 9:16.

426 Acts 3:21.

427 Genesis 1:26–2:5.

428 Joel 2:25–26.

429 Genesis 50:24–25.

430 Emily Gauvreau and Lester Cohen, *Billy Mitchell: Founder of Our Air Force and Prophet Without Honor* (Whitefish, MT: Kessinger Publishing, 2010), p. 143–156.

431 Roger G. Miller, *Billy Mitchell: "Stormy Petrel of the Air"* (Washington, DC: Office of Air Force History, 2004), p. 1.

432 Rebecca Maksel, "The Billy Mitchell Court Martial: Courtroom Sketches from Aviation's Trial of the Century," *www.airspacemag.com*, accessed 23 October 2018, https://www.airspacemag.com/history-of-flight/the-billy-mitchell-court-martial-136828592/.

433 Rebecca Maksel, "The Billy Mitchell Court Martial: Courtroom Sketches from Aviation's Trial of the Century," *www. airspacemag.com*, accessed 23 October 2018, https://www.airspacemag.com/history-of-flight/the-billy-mitchell-court-martial-136828592/.

434 Milton Sperling and Emmet Lavery, *The Court Martial of Billy Mitchell, www.imdb.com*, accessed 15 November 2019, https://www.imdb.com/title/tt0047956/, originally directed by Otto Preminger, 1955.

435 Rebecca Maksel, "The Billy Mitchell Court Martial: Courtroom Sketches from Aviation's Trial of the Century," *www.airspacemag.com*, accessed 23 October 2018, https://www.airspacemag.com/history-of-flight/the-billy-mitchell-court-martial-136828592/.

436 Rebecca Maksel, "The Billy Mitchell Court Martial: Courtroom Sketches from Aviation's Trial of the Century," *www.airspacemag.com*, accessed 23 October 2018, https://www.airspacemag.com/history-of-flight/the-billy-mitchell-court-martial-136828592/.

437 CIA, "A Look Back…The National Security Act of 1947," *www.cia.gov*, accessed 16 November 2019, https://www.cia.gov/news-information/featured-story-archive/2008-featured-story-archive/national-security-act-of-1947.html.

438 Elizabeth Howell, "Chuck Yeager: First Person to Break the Sound Barrier," *www.space.com*, accessed 16 November 2019, https://www.space.com/26204-chuck-yeager.html.

439 Acts 3:21.

440 Hebrews 12:2.

441 Exodus 31:1–5.

442 Proverbs 29:18 NASB.

443 Blue Letter Bible Institute, "Definition of Vision," Strong's Reference H2377, *www.blueletterbible.org*, accessed 17 August 2019, https://www.blueletterbible.org/lang/lexicon/lexicon.cfm?Strongs=H2377&t=NASB.

444 Blue Letter Bible Institute, "Definition of Unrestrained," Strong's Reference H6544, *www.blueletterbible.org*, accessed 8 December 2020, https://www.blueletterbible.org/lang/lexicon/lexicon.cfm?Strongs=H6544&t=NASB.

445 Habakkuk 2:2–3 NASB.

446 Proverbs 4:23.

447 Romans 16:20.

448 Philippians 4:7.

449 Romans 11:29.

450 Consulting-Specifying Engineer, "Not Everything Has Been Invented-yet," *www.csemag.com*, 23 April 2013, accessed 8 December 2020, *https://www.csemag.com/articles/not-everything-has-been-invented-yet/*.